First School Dictionary

Illustrated by
Stephanie Strickland

BARRON'S

First edition for the United States and Canada published exclusively
by Barron's Educational Series, Inc., in 2001.
Published by arrangement with HarperCollins*Publishers* Ltd

First published in 2000 by HarperCollins*Children's Books*, a division of HarperCollins*Publishers* Ltd
Copyright © 2000 by HarperCollins*Publishers* Ltd

All inquiries should be addressed to:
Barron's Educational Series, Inc.
250 Wireless Boulevard
Hauppauge, New York 11788
http://www.barronseduc.com

International Standard Book No. 0-7641-5434-6
Library of Congress Catalog Card No. 2001088821

Printed in Scotland
9 8 7 6 5 4 3 2 1

Compilers   Jock Graham, Marie Lister

Literacy consultants   Kay Hiatt, Ginny Lapage
Numeracy consultant   Jan Henley
Science consultant   Rona Wyn Davies

Cover designer   Susi Martin
Design   Perry Tate Design
Illustrators   Stephanie Strickland,
                           Sebastian Quigley (pp. 176–179)

Photos
All commissioned photos by Steve Lumb.

The publishers wish to thank the following for permission to use
photographs:
Art Directors & Trip: p. 8 airplane, p. 28 castle, p. 60
flower, p. 62 frog, p. 80 jigsaw, p. 97 moon, p. 159 tongue,
p. 174 zipper; **Biofotos/Heather Angel**: p. 72 hedgehog; **Holt
Studios**: p. 23 bud; **ICCE**: p. 50 Earth; **Oxford Scientific
Films**: p. 14 badger, p. 27 carrot, p. 61 fossil, p. 63 gerbil,
p. 83 koala, p. 89 lizard, p. 105 panda, p. 110 peacock, p. 111
penguin, p. 119 plum, p. 124 raspberries, p. 172 wolf; **Papilio**:
p. 6 acorn, p. 8 alligator, p. 10 antelope, p. 16 basket, p. 19
blackbird, p. 34 cliff, p. 34 coconut, p. 36 cookies; **Tony Stone
Images**: p. 12 astronaut, p. 30 chimpanzee, p. 39 crocodile,
p. 163 twins, p. 173 wrinkles; **John Walmsley**: p. 147 statue.

All other photos and illustrations © HarperCollins*Publishers* Ltd,
2000.

Acknowledgments
The publishers would also like to thank all the teachers, staff, and
pupils who contributed to this book:

Models
Kayla Castello   Ismael Khan
Stacey Cleary   Lindsay Linehan
Tom Crane   Guy Orridge
Katherine Davis   Zina Patel
William Davis   Thomas Permaul-Baker
Nicki Denaro and Mauri-Joy Smith   Tom Symonds
Elizabeth Fison   Lara Walters
Jesse Johnson

Schools
Aberhill Primary, Fife; ASDAC, Fife; Canning St Primary,
Newcastle upon Tyne; Cowgate Primary, Newcastle upon
Tyne; Crombie Primary, Fife; the Literacy Team at Dryden
Professional Development Centre, Gate shead; Dunshalt
Primary, Fife; Ecton Brook Lower, Northampton; English
Martyrs RC Primary, Newcastle upon Tyne; Hotspur Primary,
Newcastle upon Tyne; John Betts Primary, London; Lemington
First, Newcastle upon Tyne; Literacy Centre, Newcastle upon
Tyne; LMTC Education Development Centre, Northumberland;
Melcombe Primary, London; Methilhill Primary, Fife;
Northampton High, Northampton; Pitcoudie Primary, Fife;
Pitreavie Primary, Fife; Ravenswood Primary, Newcastle upon
Tyne; St Andrew's CE Primary, London; Simon de Senlis
Lower, Northampton; Sinclairtown Primary, Fife; Standens
Barn Lower, Northampton; Touch Primary, Fife; Towcester
Infants, Northampton; Wooton Primary, Northampton.

Contents

Using this dictionary

A **dictionary** tells you what a word means and how to spell it. The words in a dictionary are in alphabetical order.

How to find a word

Look for the word "octopus." What letter does it begin with?

guide word   new letter starts here   guide word

oak   **order**

octagon octagons
An **octagon** is a flat shape that has eight sides. (See page 188.)

October
October is the tenth month of the year. It has 31 days.

oak oaks
An **oak** is a large tree. It has seeds called acorns. Its hard wood is often used to make furniture.

octopus octopuses
An **octopus** is a sea creature. It catches food with its eight long arms.

oar oars
An **oar** is a long pole with a flat end. You pull on an **oar** to move a boat through water.

odd odder, oddest
1 An **odd** number cannot be divided exactly by two. There will always be one left over.
2 Something **odd** is a bit strange.

off
1 If you take **off** your coat, you do not wear it anymore.
2 If a light or machine is **off**, it is not switched on.
3 When you get **off** something, you are not on it anymore.
We get **off** the bus at the next stop.

oats
Oats are the seeds of a plant. They are used to make food for people and animals.

offer offers, offering, offered
If you **offer** something to someone, you ask if he or she would like it.
I offered Ronan some ice cream.

obey obeys, obeying, obeyed
When you **obey** someone, you do what they say.

office offices
An **office** is a room where people work.

ocean oceans
An **ocean** is a huge sea.

o'clock
You use **o'clock** when you say a time that is exactly on the hour.
Five **o'clock** means exactly five hours after noon or midnight.

often
Often means many times.
We often have a picnic outside in the summer.

oil oils
Oil is a smooth, thick liquid. One kind of **oil** is burned to keep people warm or used in machines. Another kind of **oil** is used for cooking food.

old older, oldest
An **old** person was born a long time ago. Something **old** was made a long time ago.

once
1 If something happens **once**, it happens one time only.
2 If something happens at **once**, it happens right away.

onion onions
An **onion** is a white or red vegetable with a strong taste.

only
Only means one or no more than.
You can **only** have one chocolate.
Gary's little – he's **only** three.
This is the **only** box I can find.

open opens, opening, opened
1 When something is **open**, it is no longer closed.
2 If you **open** something, you make it **open**.
Dad **opened** the door.

operation operations
When doctors repair a person's body, they do an **operation**.

opposite opposites
The **opposite** of something is different from it in every way.
Light is the **opposite** of dark.

orange oranges
1 An **orange** is a round, juicy fruit. It has a thick **orange** skin.

2 **Orange** is a color made from a mixture of red and yellow. (See page 188.)

orchestra orchestras
An **orchestra** is a large group of people who play musical instruments together.

order orders, ordering, ordered
1 The **order** of things is how they are arranged.
The words in this book are in alphabetical **order**.
2 If you **order** something in a restaurant, you say you would like it.
3 If you are **ordered** to do something, you must do it.

alphabet line   headword   definition   alphabet line

104   105

You can find the letter "o" in three places:
1 Each new letter starts with **big letters at the top** of the page.
2 Look at the **alphabet line** on the side of the page. This helps you remember alphabetical order, from **a** to **z**. The pink box shows you that the words on this page start with "o."
3 Look at the **guide word** at the top of each page. These are the first and last words on these pages. Here, the first word is "oak" and the last word is "order." Do these words start with the same letter as "octopus"?

When you find the right page, look at the blue words. These are called **headwords**. The headwords are in alphabetical order. Find "octopus."

Look at the **definition** under the headword. The definition tells you what the word means.

The **headword** is the word that you are looking up.

The **definition** tells you what the word means.

This word has **more than one meaning**.

Some definitions have an **example sentence**. This shows you how the word can be used.

Next to the word you will see how to spell the **plural or other forms** of the word.

Some definitions tell you **where to find out more**.

A photograph or **illustration** tells you more about what the word means.

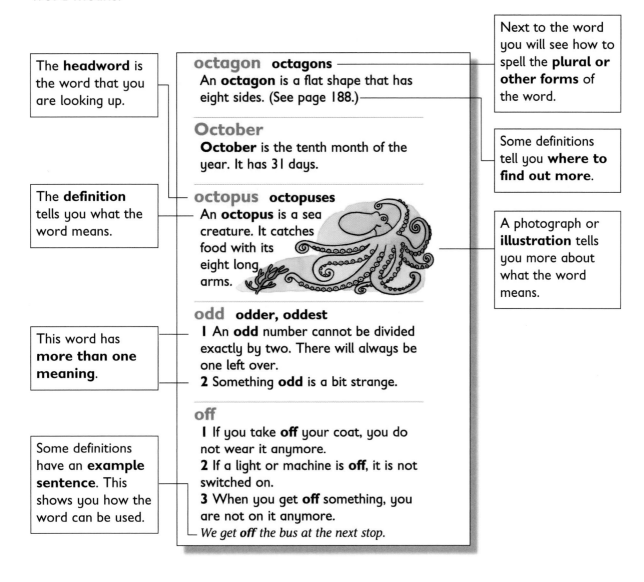

octagon   octagons
An **octagon** is a flat shape that has eight sides. (See page 188.)

October
October is the tenth month of the year. It has 31 days.

octopus   octopuses
An **octopus** is a sea creature. It catches food with its eight long arms.

odd   odder, oddest
1 An **odd** number cannot be divided exactly by two. There will always be one left over.
2 Something **odd** is a bit strange.

off
1 If you take **off** your coat, you do not wear it anymore.
2 If a light or machine is **off**, it is not switched on.
3 When you get **off** something, you are not on it anymore.
*We get **off** the bus at the next stop.*

Picture pages, word banks, and number banks

This dictionary also has special pages at the back.

Picture pages have **illustrations with labels**. Labels tell you what something is called. The labels at the back of this book tell you the names of dinosaurs, parts of the body, parts of a bicycle, parts of a car and clothes.

Word banks and number banks help you learn and spell time words, question words, synonyms and antonyms, shapes and colors.

Aa

b
c
d
e
f
g
h
i
j
k
l
m
n
o
p
q
r
s
t
u
v
w
x
y
z

abacus   abacuses
An **abacus** is a counting frame with beads that move on wires or rods.

The number of beads for this abacus shows us the size of the number. This number has 2 hundreds, 3 tens and 1 unit. It is 231.

able
When you can do something, you are **able** to do it.
*I am **able** to read this book now.*

about
1 About means to do with.
*My book is **about** Africa.*
2 About also means not exactly.
*I'll be home at **about** 6 o'clock.*

accident   accidents
An **accident** is something which happens that was not planned.
*The car slid on the ice, causing an **accident**.*
*Mom broke the cup by **accident**.*

ache   aches
An **ache** is a pain that goes on hurting, like a toothache.
*I have had an **ache** in my leg all day.*

acorn   acorns
An **acorn** is a small nut that grows on an oak tree. Oak trees grow from **acorns**.

act   acts, acting, acted
1 You **act** when you do something.
*The doctor **acted** quickly to save his life.*
2 When you pretend to be someone in a play or film, you are **acting**.

active
An **active** person is full of life and is doing something.

actor   actors
An **actor** is a man or woman who acts in a play or a film.

actress   actresses
A female actor is sometimes called an **actress**.

add   adds, adding, added
1 If you **add** one thing to another, you put it with something else.
2 If you **add** numbers, you find out how many they make altogether. The symbol + means **add**.
***Add** one and one to make two.* $1 + 1 = 2$

addition
Addition is what you do when you add numbers or other things together.

address   addresses
Your **address** is where you live.
My address is 15 Castle Street, Dover.

adjective   adjectives
An **adjective** is a word that describes a person or thing.

The little girl lived in an old house.

adjectives

adult   adults
An **adult** is a grown-up person.

adventure   adventures
You have an **adventure** when something exciting happens to you.

adverb   adverbs
An **adverb** is a word that tells you more about a verb.

The wind blew wildly.

adverb

afraid
When you are **afraid**, you are scared or frightened.

after
Something that is **after** something else is later than it.
I watch television after school.

afternoon   afternoons
The **afternoon** is the part of the day between 12 noon and evening.

again
If you do something **again**, you do it once more.
Sarah rang the bell and then she rang it again.

against
1 If you put a ladder **against** a wall, you put it so close that it touches the wall.
2 If you are playing **against** a team, you are on the other side.

age   ages
Your **age** is the number of years you have lived.

ago
Ago means in the past.
Joe started school two years ago.

agree   agrees, agreeing, agreed
When you **agree** with someone, you think the same as they do.
The girls agreed to go swimming.

air
Air is made of gases. It is all around but you cannot see it. People must breathe **air** to live.

Aa
b
c
d
e
f
g
h
i
j
k
l
m
n
o
p
q
r
s
t
u
v
w
x
y
z

Aa

b
c
d
e
f
g
h
i
j
k
l
m
n
o
p
q
r
s
t
u
v
w
x
y
z

airplane airplanes
An **airplane** is a flying machine that carries people and things.

airport airports
Airplanes land and take off at an **airport**.

alien aliens
An **alien** is a creature from another planet.
*The **aliens** arrived in a spaceship.*

alike
People or things that are nearly the same are **alike**.
*Arun and Ram look **alike** because they are brothers.*

alive
When people, animals and plants are living, they are **alive**.

all
1 **All** means each member or part.
All my family came to the wedding.
2 **All** also means the whole of something.
*Liz ate **all** the jelly.*

alligator alligators
An **alligator** is a scaly reptile that looks like a crocodile. It lives on land and in water.

alliteration
Using words which begin with the same sound closely together is called **alliteration**.
*"Green grass" is an example of **alliteration**.*

allow allows, allowing, allowed
When you **allow** someone to do something, you let them do it.
*Kate **allowed** Peter to use her ruler.*

almost
Almost means nearly but not quite.
*It was **almost** 3 o'clock.*

alone
You are **alone** if there is nobody with you.

aloud
When you read **aloud**, people can hear you.

alphabet alphabets
An **alphabet** is all the letters used in writing, set out in a special order.
There is an **alphabet** down the side of this page.

alphabetical
Alphabetical means in the same order as the letters of the alphabet.
The words in this dictionary are listed in **alphabetical** *order.*

already
Already means before now.
I have **already** *had my dinner.*

also
Also means as well.
I can swim and dive. I can **also** *skate.*

altogether
When you add things up, the answer is what you have **altogether**.
Rasheed has four stickers and Anna has five, so they have nine stickers **altogether**.

always
If something **always** happens, it happens every time.
This bus is **always** *late.*

amazing
If something is **amazing**, you are filled with a feeling of great surprise.

ambulance **ambulances**
An **ambulance** is a special van that takes sick people to the hospital.

amount **amounts**
The **amount** of something is how much of it there is.
There was a huge **amount** *of snow on the road.*

amphibian **amphibians**
An **amphibian** is an animal that lives part of its life in water and part on the land. A frog is an **amphibian**.

analog
The face of an **analog** clock or watch has numbers from 1 to 12. Two hands point to the numbers to tell you the time.

ancient
Ancient means very old or long ago.
The pyramids were built in **ancient** *times.*

angry **angrier, angriest**
If you are very annoyed and upset, you feel **angry**.

animal **animals**
An **animal** is a living creature that is not a plant. For example, dogs, birds, fish, insects, and people are **animals**.

ankle **ankles**
Your **ankle** is the part of your leg that joins your foot.
(See page 174.)

b
c
d
e
f
g
h
i
j
k
l
m
n
o
p
q
r
s
t
u
v
w
x
y
z

anniversary anniversaries
An **anniversary** is a date you remember each year because something special happened on it.
*The 25th of May is my grandparents' wedding **anniversary**.*

announce announces, announcing, announced
When you **announce** something, you say it aloud to let everyone know.
*Miss Jones **announced** the winner.*

annoy annoys, annoying, annoyed
If you **annoy** someone, you make them angry.

another
1 **Another** means one more.
*Can I have **another** cake?*
2 **Another** can also mean different.
*Try to do the sum **another** way.*

answer answers, answering, answered
1 If you **answer**, you speak to someone who has just spoken to you.
2 You give an **answer** when somebody asks you a question.

ant ants
An **ant** is a tiny insect. **Ants** live in large groups.

antelope antelopes
An **antelope** is a wild animal from Africa that looks like a deer. It can run very fast.

antonym antonyms
An **antonym** is a word that means the opposite of another word. Hot is the **antonym** of cold. Fast is an **antonym** of slow. (See page 181.)

anxious
If you are **anxious**, you are worried about something.

any
1 **Any** means one, some or a few.
*Have you got **any** chips?*
2 **Any** also means whichever you want.
*I'm not busy, so you can come **any** day.*

anybody
Anybody means any person.

anyone
Anyone is another word for anybody.

anything
Anything means any thing at all.

anywhere
Anywhere means in any place at all.
*I'll meet you **anywhere** you like.*

apart
If something falls **apart**, it falls to pieces.

ape apes
An **ape** is a monkey without a tail. Gorillas and chimpanzees are **apes**.

apologize **apologizes, apologizing, apologized**
If you **apologize**, you say you are sorry for something you have done.
Sue apologized for being late.

appear **appears, appearing, appeared**
When something **appears**, you can suddenly see it.

apple **apples**
An **apple** is a round, juicy fruit that grows on a tree. Its skin can be red, green, or yellow.

April
April is the fourth month of the year. It has 30 days.

apron **aprons**
You wear an **apron** over your clothes to keep them from getting dirty when you paint or cook.

arch **arches**
An **arch** is part of a building or bridge. It has a curved top and straight sides.

area **areas**
An **area** is a part of a country or place.
This park has a special area for dogs.

argue **argues, arguing, argued**
If you **argue** with someone, you quarrel with them.

argument **arguments**
An **argument** happens when people argue.

arm **arms**
Your **arm** is a part of your body. It is between your hand and your shoulder. (See page 174.)

armor
Armor is metal clothing or plates worn to protect the body.
Long ago, soldiers wore suits of armor.

army **armies**
An **army** is a large group of soldiers trained to fight on land.

arrange **arranges, arranging, arranged**
1 If you **arrange** to do something, you make plans to do it.
Mom and dad arranged a trip to France.
2 If you **arrange** things, you put them in order.
Lisa arranged the books in neat piles.

Aa

b
c
d
e
f
g
h
i
j
k
l
m
n
o
p
q
r
s
t
u
v
w
x
y
z

array arrays
An **array** is a group of things set out neatly in columns and rows.

arrive arrives, arriving, arrived
When you **arrive** at a place, you get there.

arrow arrows
1 An **arrow** is a thin stick with a point at one end and feathers at the other. It is shot from a bow.
2 An **arrow** is also a sign that points to something or shows you the way.

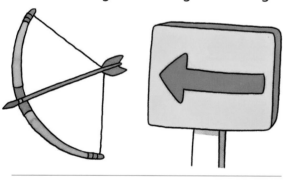

art
Art is paintings, drawings, and sculptures.
*I saw lots of pictures at the **art** show.*

ask asks, asking, asked
1 You **ask** someone a question when you want to find the answer.
*"When is the party?" Simon **asked**.*
2 You **ask** for something when you want to be given it.
*"May I have some pudding?" Amy **asked**.*

asleep
When you are **asleep** your eyes are closed. You do not know what is happening around you.

assembly assemblies
An **assembly** is a group of people meeting together.
*The judge goes to an **assembly** every day.*

assistant assistants
An **assistant** is someone who helps another person.

astronaut astronauts
An **astronaut** flies in a spacecraft and travels in space.

ate See **eat**.

atlas atlases
An **atlas** is a book of maps.

attack attacks, attacking, attacked
If you **attack** someone, you try to harm them.

attention
When you watch and listen carefully, you are paying **attention**.

attract attracts, attracting, attracted
If something **attracts** you, you become interested in it.

audience audiences
The people who watch or listen to a concert, film, or TV show are the **audience**.
*The **audience** laughed at the clowns.*

August
August is the eighth month of the year. It has 31 days.

aunt or auntie
aunts or aunties
Your **aunt** is the sister of your mother or father, or the wife of your uncle.

author authors
An **author** is a person who writes books or plays.

automatic
An **automatic** machine does things on its own.
*An **automatic** washing machine washes clothes on its own.*

autumn
Autumn is the season between summer and winter. It gets cooler and the leaves fall off many trees.

awake
When you are **awake**, your eyes are open. You know what is happening around you.

away
If you go **away**, you leave the place where you are.

awful
Awful means very bad.
*Dad had an **awful** cold.*

ax axes
An **ax** is a tool with a handle and a sharp metal edge. People chop wood with an **ax**.

baby babies
A **baby** is a very young child.

baby carriage baby carriages
You can push a baby from place to place in a **baby carriage**.

back backs
1 The **back** of something is the opposite side to the front.
2 Your **back** is the part of the body between your neck and your bottom.

backward
1 If you walk **backward**, you are walking in the direction that is behind you.
2 **Backward** is the opposite way to forward. If you say the alphabet **backward**, you start at Z and finish at A.

bacon
Bacon is a kind of meat. It comes from a pig.
*We had eggs and **bacon** for breakfast.*

bad worse, worst
1 Something **bad** is not good.
2 Food is **bad** when it is too old to eat.

badge badges
A **badge** is a small sign with words and pictures. You wear it on your clothes.

badger badgers
A **badger** is a wild animal. It has black and white fur and lives underground. It comes out at night to hunt for food.

bag bags
A **bag** is used to hold things. It can be made of cloth, plastic, paper, or leather.

bake bakes, baking, baked
When you **bake** food, you cook it in an oven.

baker bakers
A **baker** bakes and sells bread and cakes.

balance balances, balancing, balanced
1 When you **balance** something, you keep it steady and stop it from falling.

2 A **balance** is a weighing machine.
*Put these two parcels on the **balance** to see which one is heavier.*

ball **balls**
A **ball** is a round object. You can throw, catch, hit, roll, or kick it.

ballet
Ballet is a special kind of dancing. It often tells a story.

balloon **balloons**
A **balloon** is a thin rubber bag. It can be blown up to make it float in the air.

banana **bananas**
A **banana** is a long fruit. You peel off its thick yellow skin to eat it.

band **bands**
I A **band** is a group of people who play music together.
2 A **band** is also a narrow strip of something, such as a rubber band.

bandage **bandages**
A **bandage** is a strip of material. It is put over a cut to keep it clean.

bang **bangs, banging, banged**
I A **bang** is a sudden loud noise.
*The balloon burst with a **bang**.*
2 When you **bang** something, you hit or shut it noisily.
*Harry **banged** the door shut.*

bank **banks**
I People put their money in a **bank** to keep it safe.
2 A **bank** is also the land near the side of a river.

bar **bars**
I A **bar** is a long piece of wood or metal.
2 A **bar** is also something made in a rectangular shape, like a **bar** of soap or a **bar** of chocolate.

bare
I **Bare** means uncovered.
*Kim took her shoes off and danced in her **bare** feet.*
2 **Bare** can also mean empty.
*The fridge was **bare** so mom bought some more food.*

bargain **bargains**
A **bargain** is something that is worth more than you pay for it.

bark **barks, barking, barked**
I The **bark** of a tree is the hard part that covers its trunk.
2 A dog that **barks** makes a short, loud sound.

barn **barns**
A **barn** is a large building on a farm. Farmers store their crops in **barns**.

a
Bb
c
d
e
f
g
h
i
j
k
l
m
n
o
p
q
r
s
t
u
v
w
x
y
z

base

The **base** is the bottom part of something.

*The boys camped at the **base** of the mountain.*

basket   baskets

A **basket** is a container made of thin strips. It is used to store or carry things.

bat   bats

1 A **bat** is a piece of wood with a handle. It is used to hit a ball.
2 A **bat** is also an animal. It looks like a mouse with wings. **Bats** fly at night and hang upside down when they sleep.

bathrobe   bathrobes

A **bathrobe** is a piece of clothing. It is like a coat and you wear it over your night clothes. (See page 176.)

bathroom   bathrooms

A **bathroom** is the room where you wash yourself.

bathtub   bathtubs

A **bathtub** is a long container. You fill it with water and sit in it to wash your body.

battery   batteries

A **battery** is a small object that gives electricity. Watches and flashlights need the energy from **batteries** to work.

battle   battles

A **battle** is a fight between armies.

beach   beaches

A **beach** is the land at the edge of the sea. It is covered in sand or pebbles.

beak   beaks

A bird's **beak** is the hard part of its mouth.

bean   beans

A **bean** is a vegetable. There are different kinds, like red kidney **beans** and string **beans**.

bear   bears

A **bear** is a large, wild furry animal with claws. Grizzly **bears** and polar **bears** are very big and heavy.

beard **beards**
A **beard** is the hair that grows on a man's chin and cheeks.

beat **beats, beating, beat, beaten**
1 When you **beat** someone in a race, you finish before they do.
2 If you **beat** something, you hit it again and again.
*The soldier was **beating** the drum.*

beautiful
Something that is lovely to see or hear is **beautiful**.
*The sunset was **beautiful** tonight.*

because
Because is a word used to give a reason why.
*We were late **because** we missed the bus.*

bed **beds**
A **bed** is a piece of furniture you sleep on.

bedroom **bedrooms**
A **bedroom** is the room where you sleep. A **bedroom** has a bed in it.

bedtime
Bedtime is the time of day when you usually go to bed.

bee **bees**
A **bee** is an insect with wings. **Bees** make honey. Some **bees** live in beehives.

beetle **beetles**
A **beetle** is an insect. It has hard shiny wings.

before
If something is **before** something else, it happens earlier than it.
*I brush my teeth **before** I go to bed.*

begin **begins, beginning, began, begun**
You **begin** something when you start to do it.
*I always **begin** to get hungry at playtime.*

behave **behaves, behaving, behaved**
When you **behave** yourself, you are being good.

behind
If you are **behind** something, you are at the back of it.
*Lucy hid **behind** the fence.*

believe **believes, believing, believed**
When you **believe** something, you think it is true.

bell **bells**
A **bell** is something that rings when you hit, shake, or press it.
*The school **bell** rings every morning.*

belong **belongs, belonging, belonged**
When something **belongs** to you, you own it.
*This bag **belongs** to me. It has my name on it.*

a
Bb
c
d
e
f
g
h
i
j
k
l
m
n
o
p
q
r
s
t
u
v
w
x
y
z

a

Bb

c
d
e
f
g
h
i
j
k
l
m
n
o
p
q
r
s
t
u
v
w
x
y
z

belt belts
A **belt** is a long strip of leather or cloth. It is worn around the waist.

bend bends, bending, bent
1 If you **bend** something, it is no longer straight.

2 A **bend** in a road is where it goes around a corner.

berry berries
A **berry** is a small, juicy fruit that grows on bushes or trees.

best
If you are the **best**, you are better than anyone else at something.
*Pete was the **best** soccer player ever.*
See **good** and **well**.

better
1 If you do something **better** than someone, they are not as good at it as you are.
*John is good at drawing, but Roberto is even **better**.*
2 If you have been ill, you are **better** when you feel well again.
See **good** and **well**.

between
1 Something that is **between** two other things is in the middle.
*The number 22 is **between** numbers 21 and 23.*
2 If you share something equally **between** two people, you give them the same amount or number.
*Jenny and Leela shared six cookies equally **between** them. They got three each.*

bicycle bicycles
A **bicycle** is a vehicle with two wheels. You sit on it and turn the pedals with your feet.

big bigger, biggest
Big means large in size.
*This is too **big** for me now. It will fit me when I'm **bigger**.*

bike bikes
Bike is another word for bicycle.

bin bins
A **bin** is a container. You put garbage in a trash **bin**.

bird birds
A **bird** is an animal with feathers. It has two wings and two legs. Most **birds** can fly.

birthday birthdays
Your **birthday** is the day you were born on.
*My **birthday** is on the first day of August.*

bit **bits**
1 *Sam **bit** the apple.*
See **bite**.
2 A **bit** is a very small piece of something.
*The cup smashed into **bits**.*

bite **bites, biting, bit, bitten**
When you **bite** something, you use your teeth to cut or tear it.
*Sam is **biting** an apple.*

blackberry **blackberries**
A **blackberry** is a small black fruit that grows on a bush.

blackbird **blackbirds**
A **blackbird** is a common bird. The male **blackbird** has black feathers and a yellow beak. The female is brown.

blackboard **blackboards**
A **blackboard** is used in a classroom. The teacher writes on it with chalk.

blade **blades**
A **blade** is the sharp part of a knife or an ax.

blame **blames, blaming, blamed**
1 If you **blame** someone, you say that they have done something wrong.
2 If you take the **blame**, you say that something was your fault.

blanket **blankets**
A **blanket** is a piece of thick cloth. It keeps you warm in bed.

blew See **blow**.

blind **blinds**
1 A **blind** person cannot see.
2 You pull a **blind** down over a window to keep out the light.

block **blocks**
A **block** is a solid piece of something.
*Lizzie built a tower of wooden **blocks**.*

block graph **block graphs**
A **block graph** is a kind of graph. The information is shown using blocks arranged in columns.

blood
Blood is the red liquid that goes around inside your body.

blouse **blouses**
A **blouse** is a kind of shirt worn by girls and women. (See page 176.)

blow **blows, blowing, blew, blown**
1 To **blow**, send air out through your mouth and nose.
*Dad is **blowing** up the balloons for my party.*

2 When the wind **blows**, the air moves faster.

a
Bb
c
d
e
f
g
h
i
j
k
l
m
n
o
p
q
r
s
t
u
v
w
x
y
z

blunt   blunter, bluntest
When something is **blunt**, it is not sharp.

blurb
The **blurb** is the information about a book on its back cover.

boat   boats
A **boat** is a vehicle that travels across water.

body   bodies
A person's **body** is the whole of them.
*Your skin covers all your **body**.*

boil   boils, boiling, boiled
1 Water **boils** when it gets very hot. You can see bubbles and steam.
2 When you **boil** food, you cook it in **boiling** water.

bold   bolder, boldest
1 **Bold** people are brave. They are not afraid to do dangerous things.
2 **Bold** letters are dark and heavy, like the word **bold** in this sentence.

bomb   bombs
A **bomb** is a weapon. It blows things apart.

bone   bones
Bones are the hard white parts inside your body. They all join together to make your skeleton.

bonfire   bonfires
A **bonfire** is a large fire that is lit outside.

bonnet   bonnets
A **bonnet** is a kind of hat.

book   books
A **book** has pages held together inside a cover. The pages show words or pictures.

boot   boots
1 A **boot** is a kind of shoe. It covers your foot and part of your leg.
2 **To boot** means "to kick."

bored
When you are **bored,** you are not interested in what you are doing.
*Adam was **bored** because it was raining and there was nothing to do.*

boring
Something **boring** is dull and not interesting.

born
A baby is **born** when it comes out of its mother's body.

borrow   borrows, borrowing, borrowed
When you **borrow** something, you use it and give it back.
*Anil **borrows** books from the library.*

both

Both means two, not just one.
*Keep **both** hands on the handlebars!*

bottle   bottles

A **bottle** is a container for liquids. It is made of glass or plastic and is narrow at the top.
*Dad bought two **bottles** of cola for the party.*

bottom   bottoms

1 The lowest part of something is its **bottom**.
*The ball rolled down to the **bottom** of the hill.*
2 Your **bottom** is the part of your body that you sit on.

bought   See **buy**.

bounce   bounces, bouncing, bounced

When something **bounces**, it jumps back from a hard surface.

bow   bows, bowing, bowed

1 (*sounds like* **cow**)
When you **bow**, you bend over at the waist.
*Jess **bowed** to the audience.*

2 (*sounds like* **no**)
A **bow** is a kind of knot.

3 (*sounds like* **no**)
A **bow** is also a bent piece of wood used for shooting arrows.

bowl   bowls

A **bowl** is a deep dish. You can put soup or breakfast cereal in a **bowl**.

box   boxes

A **box** is a container with straight sides. It sometimes has a lid.
*Liam's shoes came in a cardboard **box**.*

boy   boys

A **boy** is a child who will be a man when he grows up.

bracelet   bracelets

A **bracelet** is a piece of jewelry that you wear around your wrist.

brain   brains

Your **brain** is inside your head and controls your body. You think and remember with your **brain**.

brake   brakes

The **brakes** of a bicycle or car make it slow down or stop. (See page 175.)

branch   branches

The **branches** of a tree grow out from the trunk.

brave   braver, bravest

A **brave** person faces danger or pain without showing fear.

bread

Bread is a food. It is made from flour and baked in an oven.
*Nick likes **bread** and peanut butter.*

break breaks, breaking, broke, broken
1 When something **breaks**, it falls into pieces.
*When mom dropped the plate, it **broke** into little pieces.*

2 When a machine is **broken**, it does not work properly.
*The TV is **broken**. I can't watch cartoons.*

breakfast
Breakfast is the first meal of the day.

breathe breathes, breathing, breathed
When you **breathe**, you take air in through your mouth and nose and then let it out again.

brick bricks
A **brick** is a block made from clay.
Bricks are used to build houses.

bride brides
A **bride** is a woman on her wedding day.

bridesmaid   bride   bridegroom

bridegroom bridegrooms
A **bridegroom** is a man on his wedding day.

bridesmaid bridesmaids
A **bridesmaid** is a girl who helps a bride on her wedding day.

bridge bridges
A **bridge** is built over a road, river or railway line so that people and vehicles can cross it.

bright brighter, brightest
Something **bright** shines strongly.

brilliant
1 A **brilliant** light or color is very bright.
2 A **brilliant** person is very clever.
3 A **brilliant** film or book is very, very good.

bring brings, bringing, brought
If you **bring** someone or something to a place, you take them with you.
*Molly is **bringing** her sister to my house.*

broke See **break**.

broken See **break**.

broom brooms
A **broom** is a brush with a long handle. It is used for sweeping floors.

brother brothers
Your **brother** is a boy who has the same parents as you do.

brought See **bring**.

brush brushes
A **brush** has a handle with lots of stiff hairs joined to it. **Brushes** come in lots of shapes and sizes. You use a **hairbrush** to make your hair neat. You use a **toothbrush** to clean your teeth. **Paintbrushes** are for painting.

bubble bubbles
1 A **bubble** is a ball of air. It is surrounded by a thin layer of liquid.
Look at Zina's lovely bubbles! She is using a soapy liquid.

2 In a cartoon, what people say is written in **speech bubbles**.

bucket buckets
A **bucket** is a container with a handle. It is made from plastic or metal.
Mai Ling filled her bucket with sand.

bud buds
A **bud** is a young flower or leaf before it opens.
In the spring, buds appear on the trees.

build builds, building, built
You **build** something when you put all its different parts together.

building buildings
A **building** has walls and a roof. Houses and schools are **buildings**. See **build**.

built See **build**.

bulb bulbs
1 The **bulb** of a plant like an onion or tulip is the round part that grows in the soil.
2 A **bulb** is also the glass part of an electric lamp. It gives out light.

bull bulls
Cows and **bulls** are large farm animals. A **bull** is the male animal.

bullet bullets
A **bullet** is a small piece of metal. It is fired from a gun.

bump bumps, bumping, bumped
1 If you **bump** into something, you knock into it suddenly.
Charlie bumped into the table and knocked over the lamp.
2 A **bump** is a swelling or lump on your body.
Rose had a bump on her head.

bumper bumpers
A **bumper** is part of a car. (See page 175.)

bunch bunches
A **bunch** is a group of things that are joined or held together.
I gave my mom a bunch of flowers. Dad bought her a bunch of grapes.

a
Bb
c
d
e
f
g
h
i
j
k
l
m
n
o
p
q
r
s
t
u
v
w
x
y
z

a
Bb
c
d
e
f
g
h
i
j
k
l
m
n
o
p
q
r
s
t
u
v
w
x
y
z

bungalow bungalows
A **bungalow** is a house with no upstairs.

burger burgers
A **burger** is a flat, round piece of cooked meat in a bun.

burglar burglars
A **burglar** goes into a building to steal things.

buried See **bury**.

burn burns, burning, burned, burnt
1 If something **burns**, it is on fire.
2 When you **burn** something, you hurt it or damage it by fire or heat.
3 A **burn** is a mark or injury caused by fire or heat.

burst bursts, bursting, burst
1 When something **bursts**, it breaks suddenly.
*The balloon **burst** with a loud bang.*
2 When somebody **bursts** into something, they do it suddenly.
*The baby **burst** into tears.*

bury buries, burying, buried
If you **bury** something, you put it in a hole in the ground and cover it up.
*The dog **buried** the bone in the garden.*

bus buses
A **bus** is a large vehicle with lots of seats. It carries people from one place to another.

bush bushes
A **bush** is a large woody plant with lots of branches.

bus stop bus stops
Buses stop at a **bus stop** to let people get on or off.

busy busier, busiest
A **busy** person has a lot to do.

butcher butchers
A **butcher** cuts up meat and sells it.

butter
Butter is a yellow food made from milk. You spread it on bread.

butterfly butterflies
A **butterfly** is an insect. It has large white or colored wings.

button buttons
A **button** is a small round object sewn onto your clothes. You push it through a buttonhole when you get dressed.

buy buys, buying, bought
You **buy** something when you pay money to get it.
*I **bought** this book with my birthday money.*

buzz buzzes, buzzing, buzzed
If something **buzzes**, it makes a humming sound like a bee.

Cc

cabbage cabbages

A **cabbage** is a vegetable with green or purple leaves.

cable cables

1 A **cable** is a bundle of wires covered in rubber that carries electricity.
2 Cable television reaches people's homes through underground wires.

café cafés

You go to a **café** to have a snack or a drink.

cage cages

A **cage** is a box or room with bars. Birds and animals are sometimes kept in **cages**.

cake cakes

Cake is a sweet food. It is made by baking a mixture of flour, eggs, sugar, and shortening.

calculate calculates, calculating, calculated

If you **calculate** something, you work it out.
Calculate the answer to 8 + 3 + 4.

calculation calculations

A **calculation** is what you do when you work something out in math.
*Can you do this **calculation** in your head?*

calculator calculators

A **calculator** is a small machine for doing calculations.

calendar calendars

A **calendar** is a list that shows the days, weeks, and months of the year.
*I marked my birthday on the **calendar**.*

calf calves

1 A **calf** is a young cow or bull.
2 Your **calf** is also the back of your leg, between your knee and your heel. (See page 174.)

call calls, calling, called

1 If you **call** a person something, you give them a name.
2 If you **call** someone or give them a **call**, you telephone them.
3 If you **call** out, you speak loudly, sometimes with pain or excitement.
4 If you **call** on someone, you go to see them.

calves See **calf**.

came See **come**.

camel camels
A **camel** is an animal that has one or two large humps on its back. **Camels** live in deserts and can travel a long way without water.

camera cameras
A **camera** is a machine that takes photographs, or film or television pictures.

camp camps, camping, camped
1 A **camp** is a group of tents or huts where people live or stay.
2 When you go **camping**, you live in a tent for a short time.

can could; cans
1 If you **can** do something, you are able to do it.
*Peter **can** touch his toes.*
2 A **can** is a metal container for liquids and food.
*Mom opened a **can** of dog food.*

canal canals
A **canal** is a strip of water for boats to travel on. **Canals** are made by people.

candle candles
A **candle** is a stick of wax with string through the middle. You burn a **candle** to give you light.

cannot
If you **cannot** do something, you are not able to do it.
*Paul **cannot** touch his toes.*

can't
Can't is short for cannot.

cap caps
A **cap** is a small hat. It has a stiff piece sticking out at the front.

capacity
The **capacity** of something is the amount that it can hold.

capital capitals
1 A **capital** letter is a letter used at the beginning of a sentence or a name. **Capital** letters are sometimes called uppercase letters.
*A, B, C, D are **capital** letters and a, b, c, d are lowercase letters.*
2 A country's **capital** is the city from which it is controlled.
*The **capital** of Italy is Rome.*

captain captains
1 The leader of a group or team is often called the **captain**.
*Rosie was **captain** of the softball team.*

2 A **captain** is also the person in charge of a ship or an airplane.

caption captions
A **caption** is the writing under a picture.

car cars
A **car** is a vehicle with four wheels and an engine. It can carry four or five people. (See page 175.)

caravan caravans
A **caravan** is a group of people, often on camels or horses, going through wild territory.

card cards
1 A **card** is a piece of stiff paper with pictures and words on it. You send **cards** to people at special times like birthdays or when they are ill.
2 Playing **cards** have pictures or numbers on them. They are used to play games.

cardboard
Cardboard is very thick, stiff paper. It is used for making boxes.

care cares, caring, cared
1 If you **care** about something, it is important to you.
2 If you **care** for something, you look after it.
*It's Peshpa's turn to **care** for the hamster.*

careful
When you are **careful**, you think about what you are doing. You try not to make mistakes.

careless
When you are **careless**, you do not think about what you are doing. You often make mistakes.

carpet carpets
A **carpet** covers floors and stairs. It is usually made from wool.

carriage carriages
A **carriage** is a vehicle that carries people. It is pulled by horses.

carrot carrots
A **carrot** is a long, orange vegetable. It grows under the ground.

carry carries, carrying, carried
If you **carry** something, you hold it and take it somewhere.

cartoon cartoons
1 In a **cartoon** film, all the pictures are drawn.
2 A **cartoon** is also a drawing that makes you laugh.

a
b
Cc
d
e
f
g
h
i
j
k
l
m
n
o
p
q
r
s
t
u
v
w
x
y
z

27

a
b
Cc
d
e
f
g
h
i
j
k
l
m
n
o
p
q
r
s
t
u
v
w
x
y
z

case cases
A **case** is a container to carry or keep things in.
I keep my CDs in a special case.

castle castles
A **castle** is an old stone building. It has thick, high walls to protect the people inside.

cat cats
A **cat** is an animal with soft fur and sharp claws. Small **cats** are kept as pets. Lions and tigers are large **cats** that live in the wild.

catch catches, catching, caught
1 If you **catch** something that is moving, you stop it and hold it.
2 If you **catch** an illness, you become ill with it.
3 When you **catch** a bus, you get on it.

caterpillar caterpillars
A **caterpillar** is a creature that looks like a worm with legs. It becomes a butterfly or a moth.

cattle
Cows and bulls kept on a farm are **cattle**. Meat called beef and milk come from **cattle**.

caught See **catch**.

cauliflower cauliflowers
A **cauliflower** is a vegetable. It has a hard white center and green leaves around the outside.

cave caves
A **cave** is a hollow place in the side of a mountain or underground.

CD CDs
A **CD** or compact disc is a flat plastic disc. It stores music, or information for use by a computer.

ceiling ceilings
A **ceiling** is the flat surface that covers the top of a room.

centimeter centimeters
Length, height, width, and distance are measured in **centimeters**. There are 100 **centimeters** (cm) in a meter.

center centers
1 The **center** is the middle point of anything.
2 A **center** is a place where people go for a special reason, like a medical **center**.

century centuries
A **century** is one hundred years.

cereal cereals
Breakfast **cereals** are foods eaten with milk. They are made from the seeds of oats, wheat, or corn.

chain chains
A **chain** is a row of rings joined together in a line. **Chains** are usually made of metal.

chair chairs
A **chair** is a seat for one person. It has a back and sometimes has arms.

chalk
Chalk is a kind of soft white rock. Sticks of **chalk** are used for writing on a blackboard.

champion champions
A **champion** is someone who has won a competition.
At the Olympics, the champions win gold medals.

change changes, changing, changed
1 If you **change** something, you make it different.
2 When you get **changed**, you put on different clothes.
3 If you give too much money to pay for something, you are given **change**.
I gave the shopkeeper too much money so he gave me some change.

channel channels
1 A **channel** is a radio or television station.
I switched over to Channel 2.
2 A **channel** is also a narrow stretch of water.

chapter chapters
A **chapter** is a part of a book.
Open your books to Chapter 3.

character characters
A **character** is a person in a story, play, or film.

charge charges, charging, charged
1 If someone **charges** you for something, they ask you to pay for it.
2 If you **charge**, you run forward, often to attack someone.
The angry elephant charged through the forest.
3 The person in **charge** of something is in control of it.
Miss Dent is in charge of the class.

chase chases, chasing, chased
If you **chase** someone, you run after him or her.

cheap cheaper, cheapest
Something **cheap** does not cost very much.

check checks, checking, checked
If you **check** something, you look at it carefully to see if it is all right.

a
b

Cc

d
e
f
g
h
i
j
k
l
m
n
o
p
q
r
s
t
u
v
w
x
y
z

checkout checkouts
A **checkout** is the place in a supermarket where you pay for your shopping.

cheek cheeks
Your **cheeks** are the soft parts on both sides of your face.
(See page 174.)

cheese cheeses
Cheese is a hard or soft food made from milk.

chemist chemists
A **chemist** is a person who works with chemicals.

cherry cherries
A **cherry** is a small round fruit with a stone in the middle. **Cherries** can be red, yellow, or black.

chest chests
1 Your **chest** is the front part of your body between your neck and your stomach. (See page 174.)
2 A **chest** is a strong box with a lid.

chew chews, chewing, chewed
When you **chew** something, you keep biting it with your teeth to break it up.
Chew your food well before you swallow it.

chick chicks
A **chick** is a baby bird.

chicken chickens
A **chicken** is a large bird kept by farmers. **Chickens** give us eggs and meat.

chicken pox
Chicken pox is an illness. You get a fever and red spots on your skin.

chief chiefs
A **chief** is the leader of a group of people.

child children
A **child** is a young boy or girl.
*The **children** are playing on the swings.*

chimney chimneys
A **chimney** is an opening in a roof above a fireplace. Smoke goes up through the **chimney** into the air.

chimpanzee chimpanzees
A **chimpanzee** is a type of African ape. **Chimpanzees** are smaller than gorillas.

chin **chins**
Your **chin** is the bottom part of your face, below your mouth. (See page 174.)

chip **chips**
1 A **chip** is a flat piece of potato fried in oil.
2 If a cup has a **chip** in it, there is a small piece missing.
3 A **chip** is also a very small piece of metal that makes a computer work.

chocolate **chocolates**
Chocolate is a sweet, brown food that often comes in a bar. Drinks, cakes, and puddings can taste of **chocolate**, too.

choose **chooses, choosing, chose, chosen**
If you **choose** something, you decide which one you want.
*I've **chosen** the biggest cake!*

chop **chops, chopping, chopped**
When you **chop** something, you cut it with a knife or ax.

chose See **choose**.

chosen See **choose**.

Christmas
Christmas is the 25th of December, when people celebrate Jesus Christ's birth. People often decorate a **Christmas** tree and give each other presents.

church **churches**
A **church** is a building where some people go to pray.

cinema **cinemas**
A **cinema** is a building where films are shown.

circle **circles**
A **circle** is a perfect round, flat shape. The letter O is a **circle**.

circular
Anything in the shape of a circle is **circular**.

circus **circuses**
A **circus** is a traveling show. It is held in a large tent. You see clowns at a **circus**.

city **cities**
A **city** is a very large place where lots of people live. **Cities** are bigger than towns.

clap **claps, clapping, clapped**
When you **clap**, you make a noise by hitting your hands together.
*The children **clapped** to show they enjoyed Ravi's story.*

class **classes**
A **class** is a group of people who learn together.

classroom **classrooms**
A class has its lessons in a **classroom**.

a
b
Cc
d
e
f
g
h
i
j
k
l
m
n
o
p
q
r
s
t
u
v
w
x
y
z

31

a
b
Cc
d
e
f
g
h
i
j
k
l
m
n
o
p
q
r
s
t
u
v
w
x
y
z

claw claws

A **claw** is the sharp curved nail of an animal.
The cat dug its claws into the sofa.

clay

Clay is a kind of earth that is used to make bricks and pots.

clean cleans, cleaning, cleaned; cleaner, cleanest

1 You **clean** something to get the dirt off it.
2 Something that is **clean** has no dirty marks on it.

clear clearer, clearest

1 Something **clear** is easy to see through, like glass.
2 When something is **clear**, it is easy to see, hear, or understand.
This book has nice clear pictures.
3 If something is **clear**, nothing covers it or gets in the way.
The road was clear of snow.

clever cleverer, cleverest

A **clever** person can do things easily and quickly.

cliff cliffs

A **cliff** is a hill with a steep side that goes straight down. **Cliffs** are usually near the sea.

climb climbs, climbing, climbed

You **climb** when you go up or down something high.
My sister Lin climbed to the very top of the tree.

clinic clinics

People go to a **clinic** for help when they are not well.
Ben's eye hurt, so he went to the eye clinic.

cloak cloaks

A **cloak** is a coat that has no sleeves.

clock clocks

A **clock** is a machine that tells you the time.

clockwise

If you go **clockwise**, you move in the same direction as the hands of a clock.

close closes, closing, closed; closer, closest

1 (*sounds like* **nose**) When you **close** something, you shut it.
2 (*sounds like* **dose**) **Close** means near.

closed
Closed means shut.

cloth   cloths
1 **Cloth** is a soft material like cotton or wool. Your clothes are made of **cloth**.
2 A **cloth** is used to clean or cover things.

clothes
You wear **clothes** to keep you warm and dry. Sweaters and jeans are **clothes**. (See page 176.)
*When I get up, I put on my school **clothes**.*

clothespin   clothespins
You use a **clothespin** when you hang something up.
*Mom uses **clothespins** to hang the wash on the line.*

cloud   clouds
You can see white or gray **clouds** floating in the sky. **Clouds** are made of very small drops of water that sometimes fall as rain.

clown   clowns
A **clown** does silly things to make people laugh. **Clowns** have painted faces and wear funny clothes.

club   clubs
A **club** is a group of people who meet often to do the same thing.
*Jane and Tom go to the swimming **club** every Friday.*

clue   clues
A **clue** helps you to solve a problem or a mystery.

coach   coaches
1 **Coach** is the least expensive class in air travel.
2 A **coach** is also someone who helps you get better at a sport or lesson.
3 A **coach** can also be a kind of carriage.

coal
Coal is a black rock that is dug out of the ground. You can burn **coal** to get heat.

coast
The **coast** is the edge of the land where it meets the sea.

coat   coats
You wear a **coat** over your other clothes when you go outside.

cobweb   cobwebs
A **cobweb** is a thin net made by a spider. It catches flies and other insects.

cocoa
1 **Cocoa** is a brown powder used to make chocolate. It is made from the seeds of a tree.
2 **Cocoa** is also a hot drink that tastes of chocolate.

a b **Cc** d e f g h i j k l m n o p q r s t u v w x y z

a
b
Cc
d
e
f
g
h
i
j
k
l
m
n
o
p
q
r
s
t
u
v
w
x
y
z

coconut coconuts

A **coconut** is a large nut with a hard hairy shell. Inside there is hard white flesh that you can eat and milky juice that you can drink.

cocoon cocoons

A **cocoon** is a small ball that a caterpillar spins. A caterpillar lives inside a **cocoon** as it changes into a butterfly or moth.

coffee

Coffee is a hot drink. You make it by pouring hot water onto a powder made from **coffee** beans.

coin coins

A **coin** is a piece of metal money.

cold colder, coldest; colds

1 When you are **cold**, you want to put on more clothes.
My feet are as cold as ice!
2 If you catch a **cold**, you feel ill and your nose runs.
Mom has a bad cold and can't stop sneezing.

collar collars

1 The **collar** of a shirt or coat is the part around the neck. It often folds over. (See page 177.)
2 A **collar** is also the band you put around the neck of a dog or cat.
My dog Lottie has her name and address on her collar.

collect collects, collecting, collected

1 If you **collect** something, you go and get it.
My dad collected the parcel from the post office.
2 When you put special things of the same kind together, you **collect** them.
I collect coins from all over the world.

color colors

Red, yellow, and blue are all **colors**. You can mix them together to get other **colors**. (See page 184.)
Green is the color you get when you mix yellow and blue.

column columns

1 A **column** is a tall, solid cylinder.
The building had lots of columns.

2 A **column** is a list of numbers or words. They go down a page one below the other.
The letters of the alphabet at the side of this page are in a column.

comb combs

A **comb** is a piece of plastic or metal with teeth. You use a **comb** to tidy your hair.

come **comes, coming, came**
1 When you **come** to a place, you arrive there.
When I came to school, the playground was nearly empty.
2 If someone asks you to **come**, they want you to go with them.

comfortable
Something **comfortable** feels nice to be in or to wear.
The chair was so comfortable that I fell asleep.

comic **comics**
A **comic** is a magazine for children. It tells stories in pictures.

comma **commas**
The punctuation mark , is a **comma**. It is used to make you stop very briefly when reading, like this, or in lists of things.
Nancy likes apples , oranges , pears, and cherries.
commas

common
If something is **common**, you often see it. The opposite of **common** is **rare**.

compact disc **compact discs**
A **compact disc** is a flat, round, plastic object. It has music or information stored on it. It is also called a CD.

compare **compares, comparing, compared**
When you **compare** two things, you see how they are the same or different.

competition **competitions**
A **competition** is a test of who is best at something.

complete **completes, completing, completed**
1 If you **complete** something, you finish it.
We completed the jigsaw puzzle.
2 If something is **complete**, there is nothing left out.
Here is a complete list of the people in my class.

computer **computers**
A **computer** is a machine that stores and finds information. It can also do calculations, play games and control other machines.

concert **concerts**
A **concert** is a musical show.
Ania sang in the school concert.

cone **cones**
A **cone** has a circular top or bottom. Its other end comes to a point.
We love to eat ice cream cones!

confused
If you feel **confused**, you are not sure what to think or do.

conjunction **conjunctions**
A **conjunction** is a word that joins two parts of a sentence together. The words *and*, *but*, and *or* are all **conjunctions**.
I like baseball and football, but I don't like swimming or basketball.

a
b
Cc
d
e
f
g
h
i
j
k
l
m
n
o
p
q
r
s
t
u
v
w
x
y
z

a
b
Cc
d
e
f
g
h
i
j
k
l
m
n
o
p
q
r
s
t
u
v
w
x
y
z

conker conkers
A **conker** is a shiny brown nut. It comes from a horse chestnut tree. You thread the nuts on string to play **conkers**.

consonant consonants
A **consonant** is any letter of the alphabet except for a, e, i, o, or u.

contain contains, containing, contained
Something **contains** the things that are inside it.
*My lunch box **contains** two sandwiches and an apple.*

container containers
A **container** is anything that you keep things in.

contents
The **contents** of something are the things inside it. The **contents page** of a book tells you what information is inside.

continue continues, continuing, continued
If you **continue** to do something, you keep on doing it.
*Please **continue** reading until you get to the bottom of the page.*

control controls, controlling, controlled
If you **control** something, you make it do what you want it to.

cook cooks, cooking, cooked
If you **cook** food, you make it ready to eat. You can fry, boil, bake, or microwave it.

cookie cookies
A **cookie** is a kind of thin, hard cake.

cool cooler, coolest
If you feel **cool**, you feel almost cold.
*On a hot day it is **cool** under the trees.*

copy copies, copying, copied
1 If you **copy** something, you make something that is exactly like it.
Copy the drawing into your book.
2 A **copy** of something looks exactly the same as it does.

corn
Corn is a vegetable with little kernels that we boil and eat.

corner corners
A **corner** is where two edges, sides, or lines meet.
*A square has four **corners**.*
*Dad waited for me at the **corner** of the street.*

correct
If your answer is **correct**, you have not made any mistakes.

corridor corridors
A **corridor** is a long, narrow passage that leads to other rooms.

cost costs, costing, cost
1 If something **costs** an amount of money, that is what you pay for it.
2 The **cost** of something is what you must pay for it.

costume costumes
You wear a **costume** when you are pretending to be someone or something else.
Tom wore a **costume** *in the school play.*

cottage cottages
A **cottage** is a small house in the country.

cotton
Cotton is cloth made from the soft white seeds of a plant.
The **cotton** *plant needs plenty of sunshine to grow.*
Mom used white **cotton** *to make my blouse.*

cough coughs, coughing, coughed
When you **cough**, you clear your throat with a sudden loud noise.

could
If you **could** do something, you are able to do it or you were able to do it.
Molly **could** *read when she was five.*
See **can**.

count counts, counting, counted
1 If you **count**, you say numbers in the right order.
You **count** *up to 100 and I'll hide.*
Count *back from 5 to 2.*
Count *forward from 5 to 9.*
2 When you **count** a group of things, you work out how many there are.

counter counters
1 A **counter** is a small round object. It is used in games that are played on a board.
2 In a small shop, you are served and pay your money at the **counter**.

counterclockwise
If you go **counterclockwise**, you move in the opposite direction to the hands of a clock.

a
b
Cc
d
e
f
g
h
i
j
k
l
m
n
o
p
q
r
s
t
u
v
w
x
y
z

a
b
Cc
d
e
f
g
h
i
j
k
l
m
n
o
p
q
r
s
t
u
v
w
x
y
z

country countries
1 A **country** is a land with its own people, language, and laws.
Australia and Spain are countries.
2 The **country** is the land away from towns. You see farms, fields, trees, and rivers in the **country**.

couple couples
1 A **couple** is two things of the same kind.
2 A **couple** is also two people who are married or going out together.
That young couple are about to get married.

cousin cousins
Your **cousin** is the son or daughter of your aunt or uncle.

cover covers, covering, covered
1 If you **cover** something, you put something else on it.
Harry covered his face with his hands.

2 A **cover** is something you put over or on another thing.
The cushion has a red cover.

cow cows
A **cow** is a large farm animal. You drink the milk that comes from **cows**.

crab crabs
A **crab** is an animal with a hard shell. It lives in the sea.

crack cracks, cracking, cracked
1 If you **crack** a plate, thin lines appear on it but it does not break.
2 A **crack** is the thin line on something that is **cracked**.
3 A **crack** is also a loud noise.

cracker crackers
1 A **cracker** is a thin baked biscuit.
2 A **cracker** is anything that makes a cracking or snapping noise, as a firecracker.

crane cranes
1 A **crane** is a tall machine for lifting heavy objects.
2 A **crane** is a tall bird with a long neck and legs. It lives near water.

crash crashes, crashing, crashed
1 When something **crashes**, it hits something else suddenly and noisily.
2 A **crash** is the noise of something **crashing**.
I heard the crash of breaking glass.
3 When a computer **crashes**, it suddenly stops working.

crawl crawls, crawling, crawled
When you **crawl**, you move along on your hands and knees.
The baby crawled across the floor.

crayon crayons
A **crayon** is used for drawing in color. **Crayons** can be colored pencils or made of wax.

cream
Cream is thick, white liquid that comes from milk.
*We had strawberries and **cream** for dessert.*

creature creatures
A **creature** is any animal.

creep creeps, creeping, crept
If you **creep**, you move slowly and quietly.
*I tried to **creep** silently up the stairs.*

crib cribs
A **crib** is a bed for a baby. It has high sides to stop the baby from falling out of it.

cricket crickets
A **cricket** is a small insect that leaps and chirps.

cried See **cry**.

cries See **cry**.

crisp crispier, crispiest
1 **Crisp** is something that is frosty and snappy.
*The autum air was very **crisp**.*
2 **Crisp** food is firm and breaks easily.
*This lettuce is nice and **crisp**.*

crocodile crocodiles
A **crocodile** is a large reptile with strong teeth. It is similar to an alligator.

crop crops
A **crop** is something that farmers grow to sell.

cross crosses, crossing, crossed; crosser, crossest
1 When you **cross** something, you go to the other side of it.
2 A little mark like x or + is a **cross**.
3 A **cross** person is angry.

crosswalk crosswalks
A **crosswalk** is a place to cross the road. There are black and white stripes on the road.

crowd crowds
A **crowd** is a lot of people in one place.

crown crowns
A **crown** is a ring of gold and jewels. Kings and queens wear **crowns** on their heads.

cruel crueller, cruellest
A **cruel** person enjoys hurting others.

crunch crunches, crunching, crunched
If you **crunch** food, you break it up noisily between your teeth.

cry cries, crying, cried
1 When you **cry**, tears fall from your eyes.
2 If you **cry** out, you shout.
3 A **cry** is a shout.

cube

a b **Cc** d e f g h i j k l m n o p q r s t u v w x y z

cube **cubes**
A **cube** is a shape with six square faces that are all the same size. Sugar is sometimes made into **cubes**.

cucumber **cucumbers**
A **cucumber** is a long, thin vegetable with dark green skin.

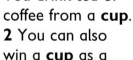

cuddle **cuddles, cuddling, cuddled**
When you **cuddle** someone, you put your arms around them.
*Dad **cuddled** the baby.*

cup **cups**
1 A **cup** is a small round container with a handle. You drink tea or coffee from a **cup**.
2 You can also win a **cup** as a prize. This kind of **cup** is made of metal.

curl **curls, curling, curled**
1 A **curl** is a piece of curved hair.
2 When you **curl** up, you bend your body into a little ball.

curtain **curtains**
A **curtain** is a piece of cloth that hangs by a window. You can pull it across to keep out the light.

curved
If a line, road, or surface bends, it is **curved**.

cushion **cushions**
A **cushion** is a bag filled with something soft. It is comfortable to lean against or sit on.

customer **customers**
A **customer** is someone who buys something in a shop.

cut **cuts, cutting, cut**
1 When you divide something with a sharp blade, you **cut** it.
*Angus **cut** his birthday cake.*
*Mom **cut** my dad's hair.*
2 If you **cut** yourself, you break open your skin and make it bleed.
3 A **cut** is an opening or wound made by something sharp.

cylinder **cylinders**
A **cylinder** is a tube with circular ends. It can be solid or hollow.

Dd

dad or **daddy** dads or daddies
Dad or **daddy** is what you call your father.

damage damages, damaging, damaged
When you **damage** something, you spoil it.
The cat scratched the chair and damaged it.

damp damper, dampest
If something is **damp**, it is a bit wet.
I've been drying my hair, but it still feels damp.

dance dances, dancing, danced
If you **dance**, you move in time to music.

danger dangers
If there is **danger**, something bad could happen.
Danger – thin ice!

dangerous
Something **dangerous** can hurt you.

dark darker, darkest
1 When it is **dark**, there is very little light or no light at all.
2 **Dark** hair is brown or black.

date dates
A **date** is the day, month, and sometimes the year when something happens.
Today's date is the 18th of September.

daughter daughters
A person's **daughter** is his or her female child.

dawn
Dawn is the early morning, when it starts to get light.
We got up at dawn to go fishing.

day days
A **day** is made up of 24 hours. There are seven **days** in a week.

dead
If someone or something is **dead**, he or it is no longer alive.

deaf
A **deaf** person cannot hear well. Some **deaf** people cannot hear at all.

dear dearer, dearest
1 When you write a letter, you put **Dear** before the person's name.
2 Something **dear** is expensive.

a
b
c
Dd
e
f
g
h
i
j
k
l
m
n
o
p
q
r
s
t
u
v
w
x
y
z

a
b
c
Dd
e
f
g
h
i
j
k
l
m
n
o
p
q
r
s
t
u
v
w
x
y
z

December

December is the twelfth month of the year. It has 31 days.

decide   decides, deciding, decided

You **decide** when you choose between two or more things.

deck   decks

A **deck** is one of the floors of a ship or bus.

*Tom sat on the top **deck** of the bus.*

decorate   decorates, decorating, decorated

1 If you **decorate** something, you make it look nice.

*Mom and I **decorated** the cake with icing.*

2 If you **decorate** a room, you paint it or paper the walls.

deep   deeper, deepest

When something is **deep**, it is a long way down to its bottom.

*Be careful! The water is very **deep** here.*

deer   deer

A **deer** is a large wild animal. The male **deer** may have horns called antlers.

defend   defends, defending, defended

If you **defend** something, you protect it.

definition   definitions

A **definition** tells you the meaning of a word. You find **definitions** in a dictionary.

*The **definition** of "baby" is "a very young child."*

delete   deletes, deleting, deleted

If you **delete** something, you cross it out or remove it.

delicious

Food that is **delicious** smells and tastes wonderful.

delighted

If you are **delighted**, you are very pleased.

*Mom was **delighted** when I won the race.*

deliver   delivers, delivering, delivered

When you **deliver** something to someone, you take it to them.

*The mail carrier **delivered** the parcel to our house.*

den   dens

1 A **den** is the home of some wild animals. Bears, foxes, and lions live in **dens**.

2 A **den** is also a room where children play or watch TV.

dentist dentists
A **dentist** looks after people's teeth.

depth
The **depth** of something is how deep it is.

describe describes, describing, described
When you **describe** something, you say what it is like.

description descriptions
The words that tell you about something are its **description**.
*Sonia gave a **description** of the burglar to the police.*

desert deserts
A **desert** is a hot, dry place. There is so little water that almost nothing grows.

desk desks
A **desk** is a special table for working on. It sometimes has drawers to keep things in.

dessert desserts
A **dessert** is fruit or a sweet food served at the end of a meal.
*We had ice cream for **dessert**.*

destroy destroys, destroying, destroyed
If you **destroy** something, you damage it so much that it can never be used again.
*The car was **destroyed** by fire.*

diagram diagrams
A **diagram** is a drawing. It shows or explains how something works.

diamond diamonds
A **diamond** is a hard bright jewel. It looks like clear glass.
*My grandma has a ring with a **diamond** in it.*

diary diaries
A **diary** is a book with a space for every day in the year. You write what happens in it.

dice
Dice are small cubes with numbers or spots on each face, usually from one to six.

dictionary dictionaries
A **dictionary** is a book that lists words in alphabetical order. It tells you how to spell them and what they mean.

did See **do**.

didn't
Didn't is short for did not.

die dies, dying, died
When people, animals, and plants **die**, they stop living.

a
b
c
Dd
e
f
g
h
i
j
k
l
m
n
o
p
q
r
s
t
u
v
w
x
y
z

difference differences

1 A **difference** between two things is what is not the same about them.
2 The **difference** between two numbers is the answer you get when you take the smaller number away from the larger number.
*The **difference** between 5 and 3 is 2.*

different

1 When two or more things are **different**, they are not the same.
2 If something is **different**, it has changed in some way.
*Your hair looks **different** – have you had it cut?*

difficult

Something **difficult** is hard to do or to understand.
*These puzzles are very **difficult**.*

dig digs, digging, dug

When you **dig** soil or sand, you use your hands or a spade to pick it up and move it.

digit digits

A **digit** is a symbol used to write numbers. There are ten different **digits** in our number system: 0, 1, 2, 3, 4, 5, 6, 7, 8, and 9.
*In the number 47, the **digits** are 4 and 7. 47 is a two-**digit** number.*

digital

A **digital** watch or clock has no hands. It gives the time in numbers.

dinner dinners

Dinner is the main meal of the day. It is sometimes the evening meal. Some people call the midday meal **dinner**.

dinnertime

Dinnertime is the time of day when you usually eat your dinner.

dinosaur dinosaurs

Dinosaurs were huge animals that lived on Earth 65 million years ago.
(See pages 172–173.)

dip dips, dipping, dipped

When you **dip** something, you put it in liquid briefly.
*Mary **dipped** her toe in the water.*

direction directions

1 If you are moving in a certain **direction**, that is the way you are going.
2 **Directions** are instructions about how to get somewhere.

dirt

Dirt is anything that makes things not clean, such as dust or mud.

dirty dirtier, dirtiest

Something **dirty** has dirt on it.
*My shoes were **dirty** after playtime.*

disappear **disappears, disappearing, disappeared**
If something **disappears**, it suddenly goes out of sight.
*The car **disappeared** around the corner.*

disappointed
You are **disappointed** when something that happens is not as good as you hoped.
*I was very **disappointed** when our team lost the match.*

disaster **disasters**
A **disaster** is something very bad that happens, causing damage and death. An air crash or an earthquake is a **disaster**.

disc **discs**
A **disc** is a flat circular piece of anything.

discover **discovers, discovering, discovered**
If you **discover** something, you find out about it or see it for the first time.

discuss **discusses, discussing, discussed**
You **discuss** something when you talk about it with other people.

disguise **disguises**
You wear a **disguise** so that people will not know who you are.
Is that Hamish wearing a disguise?

dish **dishes**
A **dish** is a plate or bowl for food.

dishwasher **dishwashers**
A **dishwasher** is a machine that washes dirty plates, cups and saucepans.

disk **disks**
Disk is another way of spelling disc.

distance **distances**
The **distance** between two things is how far it is between them.
*The **distance** between Richard and Caroline is about 3 meters.*

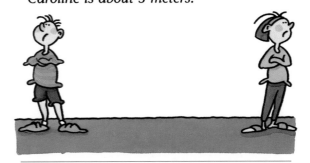

disturb **disturbs, disturbing, disturbed**
When you **disturb** someone, you stop them from doing what they are doing.
*Please don't **disturb** me – I'm trying to read.*

dive **dives, diving, dived, dove**
If you **dive**, you jump headfirst into water. You hold your arms straight above your head.
*Sadiya **dived** off the top board.*

divide divides, dividing, divided
If you **divide** something, you split it into equal groups.
*You can **divide** 6 candies into 3 groups of 2.*

6 ÷ 3 = 2

division divisions
Division is what you do when you divide numbers or things.

divorce divorces
Divorce is the separation of two persons who were married.

do does, doing, did, done
When you **do** something, you carry out an activity.
*Emma is **doing** her homework.*

doctor doctors
A **doctor** looks after people's health.

does See **do**.

doesn't
Doesn't is short for does not.

dog dogs
A **dog** is an animal that barks. **Dogs** are often kept as pets.

doll dolls
A **doll** is a toy that looks like a baby or small person.

dolphin dolphins
A **dolphin** is a mammal that lives in the sea. It looks like a fish with a large nose.

domino dominoes
A **domino** is a flat rectangular block used for playing a game. It has up to six spots on each half.

done See **do**.

donkey donkeys
A **donkey** is an animal rather like a small horse. It has long ears.

don't
Don't is short for do not.
*I really **don't** like rice pudding!*

door doors
A **door** is a piece of wood, metal, or glass that closes the way into a building, room, or piece of furniture.
*Liam opened the front **door**.*

doorbell doorbells
A **doorbell** is a bell on the outside of a house. You ring it to tell the people inside that you are there.

dot dots
A **dot** is a very small round mark.
*You put a **dot** over the letter i.*

double **doubles, doubling, doubled**
1 If you **double** something, you multiply it by two. You can also add two of the same numbers together.
6 × 2 and 6 + 6 are both ways of doubling 6.
2 If something is **double** the size, it is twice as big.

downstairs
If you go **downstairs**, you go down to a lower floor.
*Let's go **downstairs** to play.*

drag **drags, dragging, dragged**
When you **drag** something, you pull it along the ground.

dragon **dragons**
In stories, a **dragon** is a pretend animal with wings and claws. It can breathe out fire.

drain **drains**
A **drain** is a pipe to carry liquid like bath water away.

drank See **drink**.

draw **draws, drawing, drew, drawn**
1 When you **draw**, you make a picture using pencil, crayons, or chalk. You can also **draw** on a computer screen using a mouse.
2 When a game ends in a **draw**, the two sides have the same score.

drawer **drawers**
A **drawer** is a box that slides in and out of a piece of furniture. You keep things in **drawers**.

drawing **drawings**
A **drawing** is a picture made with a pen or pencil. See **draw**.

drawn See **draw**.

dream **dreams, dreaming, dreamed or dreamt**
When you **dream**, thoughts and pictures come into your mind while you are asleep.

dress **dresses, dressing, dressed**
1 When you **dress**, you put on your clothes.
2 A **dress** is a piece of clothing worn by a girl or woman. It covers her from her shoulders to her legs.

drew See **draw**.

drink **drinks, drinking, drank, drunk**
1 When you **drink**, you put liquid into your mouth and swallow it.
2 A **drink** is a liquid that you swallow.
*Would you like a **drink** of milk?*

drip **drips, dripping, dripped**
When liquid **drips**, it falls in small drops.

a b c **Dd** e f g h i j k l m n o p q r s t u v w x y z

a
b
c

Dd

e
f
g
h
i
j
k
l
m
n
o
p
q
r
s
t
u
v
w
x
y
z

drive **drives, driving, drove, driven**
1 When you **drive** a car, you make it go where you want it to.
2 A **drive** is a journey in a car.

drop **drops, dropping, dropped**
1 When you **drop** something, you let it fall.
*The dog **dropped** the stick.*
2 A **drop** is a very small amount of liquid.

drove See **drive**.

drown **drowns, drowning, drowned**
If someone **drowns**, they die under-water because they cannot breathe.

drum **drums**
A **drum** is a musical instrument that you hit to make a sound.

drunk See **drink**.

dry **drier or dryer, driest**
Something **dry** has no liquid on or in it.

duck **ducks**
A **duck** is a bird that can swim and fly. It lives near water.

dug See **dig**.

dull **duller, dullest**
1 **Dull** means not clear or bright.
2 **Dull** also means boring.

dungeon **dungeons**
A **dungeon** is a dark, underground prison beneath a castle.

dusk
Dusk is the time just before it gets dark in the evening.

dust
Dust is a dry, fine powder. It is carried on the air.

Dutch
The **Dutch** are people who live in the Netherlands.

duvet **duvets**
A **duvet** is a large cloth bag filled with something soft. You sleep under it to keep warm.

dying See **die**.

each

Each means every one of a number of things or people.
*Give **each** child two pencils.*

eagle eagles

An **eagle** is a large bird with a curved beak. It lives in the mountains.

ear ears

Your **ears** are on each side of your head. Your **ears** help you to hear. (See page 174.)

early earlier, earliest

1 If you are **early**, you arrive before you are expected.
2 The **early** part of something is near the beginning.
*I play football in the **early** morning.*

earn earns, earning, earned

You **earn** money by working for it.
*I **earned** some pocket money by washing the car.*

earring earrings

An **earring** is a piece of jewelry that you wear on your ear.

earth

1 The planet **Earth** is the world we live on.

2 The soil that plants grow in is also called **earth**.

earthquake earthquakes

When there is an **earthquake**, the ground shakes suddenly. Sometimes buildings fall down.

east

East is the direction you look to see the sun rise.

Easter

Easter is a spring festival when Christians remember Jesus Christ coming back from the dead.

easy easier, easiest

Something **easy** is simple to do or understand.
*The math was much **easier** than I expected.*

eat eats, eating, ate, eaten

When you **eat** something, you put it into your mouth and swallow it.
*I'm going to **eat** my apple at playtime.*

echo echoes

You hear an **echo** when a sound that you make comes back to you.
*Anil shouted his name in the cave and heard the **echo**.*

a
b
c
d
Ee
f
g
h
i
j
k
l
m
n
o
p
q
r
s
t
u
v
w
x
y
z

a
b
c
d

Ee

f
g
h
i
j
k
l
m
n
o
p
q
r
s
t
u
v
w
x
y
z

edge edges
1 The **edge** of something is the part furthest from its center.
My pillow fell off the edge of my bed.

2 An **edge** is where two faces of a solid object meet.
This box has 12 edges.

effort efforts
If you make an **effort**, you try very hard to do something.
Nick made a real effort to write well.

egg eggs
Baby birds, snakes, fish, and insects hatch from **eggs**. Hens lay **eggs** that people can eat.

elastic
When you pull something that is **elastic**, it stretches. When you let go, it goes back to its normal size.

elbow elbows
Your **elbow** is the middle part of your arm that bends.
(See page 174.)

electric
Something **electric** works by electricity.

electricity
Electricity is one kind of energy. It is used to give heat and light and to make machines work.

elephant elephants
An **elephant** is a very large land animal. It has a long nose called a trunk.

e-mail or email
e-mails or emails
An **e-mail** is a message that you send from one computer to another.

emerald emeralds
An **emerald** is a green jewel.

empty emptier, emptiest
If something is **empty**, there is nothing in it.
After I drank all the soda, the glass was empty.

encyclopedia encyclopedias
An **encyclopedia** is a book or CD with information on lots of different things.

end ends, ending, ended
1 The **end** of something is where it finishes.
We walked to the end of the street.
2 Something **ends** when it stops happening.
The film ends at eight o'clock.

ending endings
The **ending** is the last part of something.
The story had a sad ending.

enemy **enemies**
An **enemy** is someone who fights against you or your country.

energetic
An **energetic** person is full of life and always active.

energy
Energy is the power that makes things happen. People need **energy** to move and do things. Machines need **energy** to make them work. Electricity is one kind of **energy**.

engine **engines**
An **engine** is a machine that makes things like cars and trains move.

enjoy **enjoys, enjoying, enjoyed**
If you **enjoy** doing something, you like doing it and it makes you happy.

enormous
Enormous means very large.

enough
Something that is **enough** is as much as you need or want.
*Has Meena had **enough** to eat?*

enter **enters, entering, entered**
1 If you **enter** a place, you go into it.
2 If you **enter** something on a computer, you key it in.

entrance **entrances**
An **entrance** is the way into a place.

envelope **envelopes**
An **envelope** is a paper cover for a letter.

John Hardy
14 Victoria Road
Greentown

environment **environments**
The **environment** is the air, water, and land around us.

equal **equals, equaling, equaled**
1 If two things are **equal**, they are the same size or number.
*One week is **equal** to seven days.*
2 **Equals** means that two numbers or quantities are the same.
The symbol = means **equals**.
$5 - 1 = 4$

equipment
Equipment is the set of things needed for something or to do something.
*Bob got the camping **equipment**.*

escape **escapes, escaping, escaped**
If you **escape** something, you get away from it.
*The animals **escaped** from the burning forest.*

estimate **estimates, estimating, estimated**
1 If you **estimate** the answer to something, you make a careful guess.
2 An **estimate** is a careful guess.

even
1 If a number is **even**, it can be divided exactly by two.
2 **Even** also means flat and smooth.

a
b
c
d
Ee
f
g
h
i
j
k
l
m
n
o
p
q
r
s
t
u
v
w
x
y
z

evening evenings
Evening is the last part of the day. It starts to get dark and you go to bed.

ever
Ever means at any time.
Have you ever been to France?

every
Every means each one of a number of things or people.
Give every girl a hat and every boy a cap.

everybody
Everybody means every person.
Has everybody given me their homework?

everyone
Everyone is another word for everybody.

everything
Everything means all the things.
Have you put everything away?

everywhere
Everywhere means every place.
The dog followed her everywhere.

evil
An **evil** person is very bad.

exact
An **exact** answer cannot be any better or closer.

exactly
If you say a number or time **exactly**, it is not less or more than that.
I cut the cake into exactly three pieces.

example examples
You use an **example** to show what you mean.
Tom's picture is a good example of how to use paint.

excellent
Something **excellent** is very good.
Gill's work was excellent.

except
Except means not including someone or something.
Everyone got a candy except me.

exchange exchanges, exchanging, exchanged
If you **exchange** something, you give it away and receive something else instead.
I exchanged my book for a different one.

excited
If you are **excited**, you are so happy that you want to jump around.
I'm really excited about my birthday!

exclaim   exclaims, exclaiming, exclaimed

If you **exclaim**, you cry out suddenly.
*"Ouch! That hurt!" Dad **exclaimed**.*

exclamation mark
exclamation marks

A mark like ! is an **exclamation mark**. It is used to show that someone exclaims.
I can't wait until my birthday!

excuse   excuses

An **excuse** is a reason you give for doing or not doing something.
*You're late. What is your **excuse**?*

exercise   exercises

I Exercise is anything active that you do to keep fit.

2 An **exercise** is a set of questions that help you practice something.
*Practice your tables by doing **Exercise** 5 for homework.*

exit   exits

An **exit** is a way out of a place.
*The **exit** is blocked and I can't get out.*

expect   expects, expecting, expected

If you **expect** something to happen, you believe it will happen.
*Dan's the fastest, so I **expect** him to win.*

expensive

Something **expensive** costs a lot.

explain   explains, explaining, explained

If you **explain** something, you say what it means or why it happened.

explanation   explanations

An **explanation** says what something means or why it happened.

explode   explodes, exploding, exploded

When something **explodes**, it blows up into small pieces with a loud bang.

explore   explores, exploring, explored

If you **explore** a place, you look around to see what it is like.

expressway   expressways

An **expressway** is a highway with many lanes. People going a long way often use an **expressway**.

extinct

An animal that is **extinct** has died out. There will never be any more of them.
*Dinosaurs are **extinct**.*

extra

Something **extra** is more than usual.
*My mom gave me **extra** pocket money.*

eye   eyes

Your **eyes** are parts of your face. You see with your **eyes**.
(See page 174.)

a b c d Ee f g h i j k l m n o p q r s t u v w x y z

53

a
b
c
d
e
Ff
g
h
i
j
k
l
m
n
o
p
q
r
s
t
u
v
w
x
y
z

Ff

face   faces
1 Your **face** is the front of your head. (See page 174.)
2 A **face** of a solid object is any one of its surfaces.
A cube has six faces.

fact   facts
A **fact** is something that is true.
It is a fact that the Earth goes around the Sun.

factory   factories
Things are made in a **factory**, usually using machines.

fail   fails, failing, failed
You **fail** if you try to do something but cannot do it.
I tried to pass the test, but I failed.

fair   fairer, fairest; fairs
1 A **fair** person treats everyone the same.
2 A person who is **fair** is beautiful.
"Mirror, mirror, on the wall,
Who is the fairest of them all?"
3 Someone with **fair** hair has pale hair.
4 A **fair** is an outdoor show that moves from town to town.
I went on an exciting ride at the fair.

fairy   fairies
In stories, a **fairy** is a very small person. **Fairies** have wings and magic powers.
Zina is dressed as a fairy.

fairy tale   fairy tales
A **fairy tale** is a story where magical things happen.

fall   falls, falling, fell, fallen
1 If something **falls**, it drops toward the ground.
The apples fell from the tree onto the grass.
2 If you **fall** asleep, you go to sleep.
3 **Fall** is the season between summer and winter.

false
Something is **false** when it is not true or is not real.
The clown wore a false nose.

family   families
Your parents, brothers, sisters, grandparents, aunts, uncles and cousins are your **family**.

famous
Someone **famous** is very well known.
J. K. Rowling is a famous writer.

fantastic
If you say something is **fantastic**, you mean that it is wonderful.

far   farther or further, farthest or furthest
Far means a long way.
Are you going far?

farm farms

A **farm** is a place in the country where a farmer grows food or keeps animals.

farmer farmers

A **farmer** lives on a farm. **Farmers** grow food and look after animals.

fast faster, fastest; fasts, fasting, fasted

1 Something **fast** moves very quickly.
2 If you **fast**, you do not eat any food.

fasten fastens, fastening, fastened

When you **fasten** something, you fix one thing firmly to another.
*Please **fasten** your seat belt.*

fat fatter, fattest

1 A **fat** person or animal has a round, heavy body.
*Our dog is **fat**. She can't fit into her doghouse.*
2 **Fat** is a food. Butter is a kind of **fat**.

father fathers

A **father** is a man who has a son or daughter.

fault

It is your **fault** if you cause something bad to happen.
*It's John's **fault** the plant died, because he forgot to water it.*

favorite

Your **favorite** is the one you like best.
*Blue is my **favorite** color.*

fax faxes

You use a **fax** to send a copy of a letter or picture to someone.

fear fears, fearing, feared

1 If you **fear** someone or something, they frighten you.
2 **Fear** is the feeling you get when you are afraid.
*My mom has a **fear** of spiders.*

feast feasts

A **feast** is a large, special meal for lots of people.

feather feathers

Feathers cover the body of a bird. They are very light.

February

February is the second month of the year. It usually has 28 days. In a leap year, it has 29 days.

feed feeds, feeding, fed

When you **feed** a person or animal, you give them food.
*Did you **feed** the dog?*

feel feels, feeling, felt

1 When you **feel** happy, you are happy at that moment.
2 When you touch something to find out what it is like, you **feel** it.

feet See foot.

a
b
c
d
e
Ff
g
h
i
j
k
l
m
n
o
p
q
r
s
t
u
v
w
x
y
z

55

a
b
c
d
e

Ff

g
h
i
j
k
l
m
n
o
p
q
r
s
t
u
v
w
x
y
z

fell See **fall**.

felt See **feel**.

female females
A **female** person or animal can be a mother. Girls and women are **females**.

fence fences
A **fence** is a kind of wall around a garden or field. It is made from wood or wire.

ferry ferries
A **ferry** is a kind of boat. It carries people and vehicles across a river or a narrow piece of sea.

festival festivals
1 A **festival** is a number of special shows. A **festival** is often held every year.
2 A **festival** is also a special time, like Christmas.
*We all bring fruit and vegetables to school for our Harvest **Festival**.*

fetch fetches, fetching, fetched
If you **fetch** something, you go and get it from another place.
*I **fetched** my bike from the shop.*

fever fevers
A **fever** is an illness that makes you very hot.

few fewer, fewest
Few means not many.
*There are only a **few** seats left.*

fiction
Fiction is stories that have been made up about people or animals that are not real.

field fields
A **field** is a piece of land on a farm. It has a fence or hedge around it.

fierce fiercer, fiercest
A **fierce** animal is very angry and likely to attack.
*The **fierce** dog barked angrily.*

fight fights, fighting, fought
When people or animals **fight**, they try to hurt each other.

figure figures
A **figure** is another word for a number or an amount.

fill fills, filling, filled
When you **fill** something, you use up the space inside it.
*Mom **filled** my glass with orange juice.*

film films
1 A **film** is a story shown on a screen using moving pictures.

2 You put a roll of **film** in your camera to take pictures.

fin **fins**
A **fin** is part of a fish. It helps the fish to travel through the water.

find **finds, finding, found**
1 When you see something that you are looking for, you **find** it.
2 When you **find** out about something, you learn something new.
*Today we are going to **find** out about the weather.*

fine **finer, finest**
1 Something that is **fine** is very good.
*A **fine** day is sunny and dry.*
2 Fine can also mean that something is very thin, like a line or a thread.

finger **fingers**
You have five **fingers** on each hand. (See page 174.)

finish **finishes, finishing, finished**
When you **finish** something, you come to the end of it, use it up or do the last part of it.

fire **fires**
1 Fire is the heat and light given off when things burn.
2 People have a **fire** to keep warm.

fire brigade **fire brigades**
A **fire brigade** is a group of firefighters. People call the **fire brigade** to put out a dangerous fire.

fire engine **fire engines**
A fire brigade travels in a **fire engine**.

firefighter **firefighters**
A **firefighter** puts out dangerous fires.

firework **fireworks**
When someone lights a **firework**, it sends out bright, colored lights.

firm **firmer, firmest**
Something that is **firm** does not move easily when you push it.

first
When someone or something is **first**, he or it comes before all the others.
*January is the **first** month of the year.*

fish **fish or fishes**
A **fish** is an animal that lives under water. **Fish** are covered with scales.

a
b
c
d
e

Ff

g
h
i
j
k
l
m
n
o
p
q
r
s
t
u
v
w
x
y
z

fisherman **fishermen**
A **fisherman** is someone who catches fish.

fit **fits, fitting, fitted; fitter, fittest**
1 If something **fits**, it is the right size and shape.
2 If you are **fit**, you feel healthy and well.

fix **fixes, fixing, fixed**
1 If you **fix** something that was broken, you repair it.
*Dad managed to **fix** his car.*
2 If you **fix** something that was wrong, you adjust it.

flag **flags**
A **flag** is a rectangle of cloth with a colored pattern on it. It flies from a pole. Every country in the world has its own **flag**.

flame **flames**
A **flame** is a hot, bright tongue of fire.

flap **flaps, flapping, flapped**
To **flap** is to move the wings, or anything that looks like wings, up and down.
*The bird **flapped** its wings.*

flash **flashes**
A **flash** is a short, sudden, bright light.
*A **flash** of lightning lit up the sky.*

flashlight **flashlights**
A **flashlight** is a light you can carry.

flat **flatter, flattest; flats**
1 A **flat** surface has no bumps or slopes.
2 When some food lacks flavor, we say it is **flat**.

flavor **flavors**
The **flavor** of food or drink is what it tastes like.
*I love ice cream – chocolate is my favorite **flavor**.*

flew See **fly**.

flies See **fly**.

flip **flips, flipping, flipped**
If you **flip** something, you turn it quickly and suddenly.
*Nadia **flipped** over the page.*

float **floats, floating, floated**
1 Something that **floats** in a liquid does not sink. It stays on top.
*The plastic duck **floated** on the water.*

2 Something that **floats** through the air moves slowly without getting lower.
*The balloon **floated** across the sky.*

flock **flocks**
A **flock** is a group of birds, sheep, or goats.
*A **flock** of birds flew overhead.*

flood floods
There is a **flood** when water covers an area that is usually dry.
Boats came to rescue people from the flood.

floor floors
1 The **floor** of a room is the part you walk on.
I have a blue carpet on my bedroom floor.
2 A **floor** is all the rooms on the same level in a building.
Grandma's apartment is on the sixth floor.

floppy disk floppy disks
A computer can store information on a **floppy disk**.

flour
Flour is a white or brown powder made from wheat. It is used to make bread and cakes.

flow flows, flowing, flowed
If a liquid **flows**, it moves from place to place.
A river flows through our town.

flower flowers
A **flower** is a part of a plant. It makes seeds. Some **flowers** have colored petals.

fly flies, flying, flew, flown
1 If you **fly**, you travel through the air.
2 A **fly** is a small flying insect.

fog
Fog is thick cloud that is near the ground. It makes it difficult to see.

foggy
When it is **foggy**, it is difficult to see because of the fog.

fold folds, folding, folded
If you **fold** something, you bend it over on itself.
Susan folded up her towel.

follow follows, following, followed
If you **follow** someone, you move along behind them.
We all followed Emma to the hall.

food foods
Food is anything that people and animals eat to stay alive. **Food** gives you the energy to do things.
My favorite food is fish sticks.

foot feet
1 Your **foot** is at the end of your leg. (See page 174.)
2 A **foot** is a way to measure the length of things.

football footballs
Football is a game played by two teams. They try to pass or carry a **football** over the goal line.
My brother and I play football all day.

a b c d e **Ff** g h i j k l m n o p q r s t u v w x y z

footprint footprints
Footprints are the marks your feet leave when you walk in snow or wet sand.

forehead foreheads
Your **forehead** is the top of your face. (See page 174.)

foreign
Something that is **foreign** comes from another country.
*My family eats **foreign** food from all over the world.*

forest forests
A **forest** is a place where lots of trees grow together.

forgave See **forgive**.

forget forgets, forgetting, forgot, forgotten
If you **forget** something, you do not remember it.
*I **forgot** it was mom's birthday.*

forgive forgives, forgiving, forgave, forgiven
If you **forgive** someone, you stop being angry with them.
*Mom **forgave** me for breaking her watch.*

forgot See **forget**.

forgotten See **forget**.

fork forks
A **fork** is a tool with sharp points and a handle. You use a **fork** to help you eat your food.

fortnight fortnights
A **fortnight** is the same as two weeks.

forward
1 If you walk **forward**, you are going in the direction that is in front of you.
2 **Forward** is the opposite way to backward. If you say the alphabet **forward**, you start at A and finish at Z.

fossil fossils
A **fossil** is a plant or animal that has turned to stone. A **fossil** has been in the ground for many thousands of years.

fought See **fight**.

found See **find**.

fountain fountains
A **fountain** is a jet of water that shoots up into the air.

fox foxes
A **fox** is a wild animal that looks like a dog. It has a thick tail.

fraction fractions

A **fraction** is part of a whole number or shape. A half ($\frac{1}{2}$) and a quarter ($\frac{1}{4}$) are both **fractions**.

$\frac{1}{2}$ $\frac{1}{4}$

frame frames

A **frame** is the wood, metal, or plastic around a picture or a window.

freckle freckles

Freckles are tiny brown spots on a person's skin.

free

1 If you are **free**, you can choose where you go and what you do.
2 Something that is **free** does not cost any money.
*The supermarket gave away **free** balloons.*

freeze freezes, freezing, froze, frozen

1 Water **freezes** when it gets very cold. It changes from water into ice.
2 If you are **freezing**, you are very, very cold.

fresh fresher, freshest

1 When something is **fresh**, it is new and clean.
*Turn to a **fresh** page.*
2 **Fresh** food is not old or bad.
3 **Fresh** water is not salty from the sea. It is rainwater that has collected in a river or lake.

Friday Fridays

Friday is the day of the week between Thursday and Saturday.

fridge fridges

A **fridge** is a machine that keeps food cold and fresh. **Fridge** is short for refrigerator.

fried See **fry**.

friend friends

A **friend** is a person you know well and like very much.
*I play with my best **friend** every day.*

friendly friendlier, friendliest

A **friendly** person is kind and easy to get along with.

fries

Fries are fried potatoes. See **fry**.

frighten frightens, frightening, frightened

1 If you **frighten** someone, you make them afraid.
2 If you are **frightened**, you feel afraid.
*My dog is **frightened** of loud noises.*

frog frogs

A **frog** is a small animal that can swim and jump. **Frogs** live on land and in water.

a b c d e **Ff** g h i j k l m n o p q r s t u v w x y z

a
b
c
d
e

Ff

g
h
i
j
k
l
m
n
o
p
q
r
s
t
u
v
w
x
y
z

front
The **front** of something is the part that you usually see first.
*The driver sits at the **front** of the bus.*

frost   frosts
There is a **frost** when it gets very cold. The ground is covered with thin white ice called **frost**.

frown   frowns, frowning, frowned
When you **frown**, you look angry or worried. Lines appear on your forehead.
*Mom **frowned** when I banged the door.*

froze   See **freeze**.

frozen   See **freeze**.

fruit   fruit or fruits
Fruit is the part of a plant that holds the seeds. Apples, oranges, and bananas are **fruit** that you eat.

fry   fries, frying, fried
If you **fry** food, you cook it in hot oil or fat.

full   fuller, fullest
If something is **full**, there is no space left inside it.
*The bucket is **full** of sand.*

full stop   full stops
A **full stop** requires slowing down a car until it does not move.
*A red light demands a **full stop**.*

fun
When you have **fun**, you have a good time.
*We had a lot of **fun** at the circus.*

funny   funnier, funniest
1 Something **funny** makes you laugh.
*The clowns were really **funny**.*
2 If something is **funny,** it can be strange in some way.
*Will gave me a **funny** look.*

fur
Fur is the thick, soft hair that grows on the bodies of animals. Bears, rabbits, and cats have **fur**.

furniture
Chairs, tables and beds are **furniture**.

furry   furrier, furriest
Something **furry** is covered with thick, soft hair.

further
Further is another word for farther.
See **far**.

furthest
Furthest is another word for farthest.
See **far**.

future
The **future** is the time that has not come yet.
*Yesterday was in the past, and tomorrow is in the **future**.*

garden gardens
A **garden** is a piece of land next to a house. People grow flowers and vegetables in their **gardens**.

gas gases
1 **Gas** is something that is not solid or liquid. Air is a **gas**.
2 Many people burn **gas** to heat their homes and cook their food.

gasoline
People put **gasoline** in a car to make the engine work.

gate
A **gate** is a kind of door in a fence or wall.

gather gathers, gathering, gathered
When you **gather** things, you bring them together in one place.
The teacher gathered up the books.

gave See **give**.

geese See **goose**.

gentle gentler, gentlest
If you are **gentle**, you are kind and careful.
The nurse was very gentle with the baby.

gentleman gentlemen
Gentleman is a polite word for a man.

gale gales
A **gale** is a very strong wind.
The fence was blown down in the gale.

game games
A **game** is something you play for fun, like hide-and-seek. Sports like football are **games** – so is a board **game** like Monopoly.

gap gaps
A **gap** is an empty space between two things.
Mike has a gap where his tooth fell out.

garage garages
1 A **garage** is a building where you keep a car.
2 You also buy gasoline and have your car fixed at a **garage**.

garbage
Garbage is the things that you throw away.

a b c d e f **Gg** h i j k l m n o p q r s t u v w x y z

63

a
b
c
d
e
f
Gg
h
i
j
k
l
m
n
o
p
q
r
s
t
u
v
w
x
y
z

gerbil gerbils

A **gerbil** is a small animal that looks like a mouse. **Gerbils** are often kept as pets.

get gets, getting, got

If you **get** something, you fetch it from somewhere.
*It's cold, so I'll **get** my sweater.*

ghost ghosts

Some people believe that a **ghost** is the soul of a dead person. Some people say they have seen a **ghost**.

giant giants

1 In fairy tales, a **giant** is a very large, strong person.
2 Something very big is called **giant**.
*This is a **giant** box of cornflakes.*

gigantic

Something **gigantic** is very, very large.
*The boys ate a **gigantic** meal.*

giggle giggles, giggling, giggled

If you **giggle**, you keep on laughing.
*We couldn't stop **giggling** – it was such a good joke!*

giraffe giraffes

A **giraffe** is a tall animal with a very long neck.

girl girls

A **girl** is a child who will grow up to be a woman.
*Your mom used to be a **girl**.*

give gives, giving, gave, given

If you **give** something to someone, you let them have it.
*Sam **gave** Raul an apple.*

glad

When you are **glad**, you are pleased and happy.
*I'm really **glad** grandma's coming to stay.*

glass glasses

1 Glass is a hard, clear material that you can see through. Windows and bottles are made of **glass**.
2 A **glass** is a kind of cup made of **glass**.

glasses glasses

You wear **glasses** to help you see better. You look through two special pieces of glass or plastic held in a frame.

gloomy gloomier, gloomiest

1 If you are **gloomy**, you feel sad.
2 Gloomy weather is cloudy and rather dark.

glove gloves
You wear **gloves** on your hands to keep them warm. **Gloves** have a separate part for each finger.

glue
You use **glue** to stick things together.
*Ben stuck the picture in his book with **glue**.*

go goes, going, went, gone
If you **go** somewhere, you move from one place to another.
*My brother and I are **going** to the swimming pool.*

goal goals
1 You must put the ball in the **goal** to score a point in a game like soccer.
The crowd roared when the ball shot into the goal.
2 You score a **goal** by putting the ball into the **goal**.
*Mark scored a **goal** with a brilliant header.*

goat goats
A **goat** is a farm animal. **Goats** are kept for their milk.

gold
Gold is a shiny yellow metal. It is used to make jewelry.

golden
Something **golden** is the color of gold.
*Goldilocks had **golden** hair.*

goldfish goldfish
A **goldfish** is a small golden or orange fish. People keep **goldfish** as pets.

gone See **go**.

good better, best
1 If you think something is **good**, you like it.
*That was a **good** game!*
2 If you are **good** at something, you can do it well.
*Jack is very **good** at reading.*
3 A **good** person is kind to others and cares about them.

good-bye
You say **good-bye** to people when you leave them.

good night
You say **good night** to someone who goes to bed.

goose geese
A **goose** is a large bird that swims and flies.

a
b
c
d
e
f
Gg
h
i
j
k
l
m
n
o
p
q
r
s
t
u
v
w
x
y
z

gorilla **gorillas**
A **gorilla** is the largest ape. It has thick black fur and is very strong.

got See **get**.

grab **grabs, grabbing, grabbed**
If you **grab** something, you take hold of it quickly.
Grab your things! We're going swimming.

gram **grams**
You can measure mass in **grams**. There are 1000 **grams** (g) in a kilogram (kg).

grammar
Grammar is the rules of a language. It tells you how words and sentences should be put together.

grandfather **grandfathers**
Your **grandfather** is the father of your father or mother.

grandma **grandmas**
Grandma is another word for grandmother.

grandmother **grandmothers**
Your **grandmother** is the mother of your father or mother.

grandpa **grandpas**
Grandpa is another word for grandfather.

grape **grapes**
A **grape** is a juicy fruit that grows in a bunch.

grapefruit **grapefruits**
A **grapefruit** is a juicy yellow fruit like a big orange. People eat **grapefruit** for breakfast.

graph **graphs**
A **graph** is a special kind of drawing or diagram that shows information.

grass
Grass is a plant with thin green leaves. It grows in fields and gardens. Cows and other animals eat **grass**.

great **greater, greatest**
1 **Great** means very good.
*We had a **great** time at the fair!*
2 **Great** also means very large.
*There's a **great** black cloud up above us.*
3 **Great** can also mean important or famous.
*Lincoln was a **great** president.*

greedy **greedier, greediest**
A **greedy** person takes more than he or she needs.

grew See **grow**.

groan **groans, groaning, groaned**
If you **groan**, you make a long, low sound. You **groan** when something hurts or upsets you.
Mom groaned when she saw the mess.

ground
1 The **ground** is what you walk on.
The plane hit the ground with a crash.
2 **Ground** also means earth or land.
The ground was too hard to dig.

group **groups, grouping, grouped**
1 A **group** of people or things is a number of them that are all together.
2 If you **group** people or things, you put them together.

grow **grows, growing, grew, grown**
When something **grows**, it gets bigger.

growl **growls, growling, growled**
A **growl** is a deep, rough, angry sound made in the throat.
The lion growled angrily.

grown See **grow**.

grown-up **grown-ups**
A **grown-up** is a person who is not a child. **Grown-ups** are called adults.

guard **guards, guarding, guarded**
1 If you **guard** something, you watch over it to keep it safe.
2 A **guard** is a person who **guards** someone or something.

guess **guesses**
If you give an answer when you are not sure it is right, you are making a **guess**.

guide **guides, guiding, guided**
1 If you **guide** people, you show them the way to go.
2 A **guide** shows you around somewhere, or leads the way.
We followed the guide through the jungle.

guinea pig **guinea pigs**
A **guinea pig** is a small, furry animal without a tail. It is often kept as a pet.

guitar **guitars**
A **guitar** is a musical instrument with strings. You play it with your fingers.

gun **guns**
A **gun** is a machine that fires bullets.

a b c d e f **Gg** h i j k l m n o p q r s t u v w x y z

a
b
c
d
e
f
g
Hh
i
j
k
l
m
n
o
p
q
r
s
t
u
v
w
x
y
z

Hh

had See **have**.

hail
Hail is drops of hard, icy rain.
*The **hail** bounced off the road.*

hair **hairs**
Your **hair** is what grows on your head. It is made up of lots of **hairs**.
*Stacey has curly red **hair**.*

hairy **hairier, hairiest**
Something covered in hair is **hairy**.

half **halves**
1 If you divide something equally into two, each part is a **half**.
2 When you say the time, **half** past means 30 minutes past.
*Mom's coming home at **half** past two.*

halfway
If you are **halfway** between two places, you are the same distance from each of them.

hall **halls**
1 The **hall** of a house is just inside the front door.
2 A **hall** can also be a large room or building.
*The party was held in the school **hall**.*

Halloween
Halloween is the 31st of October. Children like to dress up in costumes.

halve **halves, halving, halved**
If you divide something exactly in two, you **halve** it.

halves See **half**.

hammer **hammers**
A **hammer** is a tool used for hitting nails into wood.

hamster **hamsters**
A **hamster** is a small, furry animal that looks like a mouse without a tail. It is often kept as a pet.

hand **hands, handing, handed**
1 Your **hand** is at the end of your arm. (See page 174.)
2 If you **hand** something to someone, you give it to them.

hand truck **hand trucks**
A **hand truck** has wheels and a handle. You use it to move heavy things.

handle   handles
The **handle** of anything is the part that you hold in your hand.
*Alice turned the **handle** and opened the front door.*

handlebars
Handlebars are part of a bicycle. (See page 175.)

handwriting
Your **handwriting** is the writing you do with a pen or pencil.

hang   hangs, hanging, hung
If you **hang** something, you hold it at the top.
*Please **hang** your coat.*

Hanukkah or Chanukah
Hanukkah is an eight-day Jewish festival of lights.

happen   happens, happening, happened
If something **happens**, it takes place.

happy   happier, happiest
When you are **happy**, you are very pleased.
*I was so **happy** on my birthday!*

harbor   harbors
Boats are tied up in a **harbor** to keep them safe from big waves.

hard   harder, hardest
1 Something that is **hard** is firm or difficult to break.
*This ice cream is as **hard** as a rock!*
2 Something that is **hard** to do is difficult.
*I can't do this puzzle – it's really **hard**!*

hare   hares
A **hare** is an animal that looks like a large rabbit. It has long ears and long back legs.

harvest   harvests
The **harvest** is the gathering of crops when they are ripe.
*At **harvest** time, the corn is cut and taken to the barn.*

has   See **have**.

hat   hats
A **hat** is something you wear on your head.

hatch   hatches, hatching, hatched
When a baby bird **hatches**, it comes out of its egg.

hate   **hates, hating, hated**
If you **hate** something, you do not like it at all.

have   **has, having, had**
1 If you **have** something, you own it or it is with you.
*Fred **has** a new bike.*
2 If you **have** done something, you did it in the past.
*I **have** been on an airplane before.*

haven't
Haven't is short for have not.
*I **haven't** done it yet – I'll do it tomorrow.*

hay
Hay is dry grass that is used to feed animals.

head   **heads**
1 Your **head** is the top part of your body. (See page 174.)
2 The **head** of something is the person in charge.
*The department **head** called everyone into the hall.*

headache   **headaches**
A **headache** is a pain in the head that goes on hurting.

headlight   **headlights**
Headlights are the lights at the front of a car. (See page 175.)

heal   **heals, healing, healed**
When something **heals**, it becomes healthy again.

healthy   **healthier, healthiest**
If you are **healthy**, your body is fit and you are not ill.

hear   **hears, hearing, heard**
When you **hear** something, you notice the sound it makes.
*I can **hear** music.*

heart   **hearts**
Your **heart** is inside your chest. It sends blood around your body.

heat   **heats, heating, heated**
1 If you **heat** something, you make it warmer.
*I'll **heat** some soup for lunch.*
2 **Heat** is the warm feeling you get from something hot.

heaven
Heaven is a place of happiness. Some people think you go to **heaven** when you die.

heavy   **heavier, heaviest**
A person or thing that is **heavy** weighs a lot.

hedge   **hedges**
A **hedge** is a kind of fence between fields or gardens. It is made of small trees and bushes.

hedgehog hedgehogs
A **hedgehog** is a small brown animal with sharp spines on its back. It rolls into a ball when it is frightened.

heel heels
1 Your **heel** is the back part of your foot. (See page 174.)
2 A **heel** is also part of a shoe.

height heights
You measure how high something is to find out its **height**.

held See **hold**.

helicopter helicopters
A **helicopter** is a vehicle that flies. It has large blades on top that spin around. **Helicopters** can go straight up into the air.

helmet helmets
A **helmet** is a hard hat that keeps your head from getting hurt.
*You should always wear a **helmet** when you ride your bike.*

help helps, helping, helped
When you **help** someone, you do something useful for them.
*I **helped** Dad carry the bags.*

hen hens
A **hen** is a female chicken. **Hens** lay eggs that people can eat.

her
Her means belonging to a girl or woman.
*Mom's coming. I can see **her** car.*

herd herds, herding, herded
1 A **herd** is a group of animals of one kind that live together.
*There is a large **herd** of cows on this farm.*

2 If you **herd** animals or people, you move them together as a group.
*The dogs **herded** the sheep into a corner.*

here
Here means the place where you are now.
*Have you seen my skateboard? I thought I left it **here**.*

hero heroes
1 A **hero** is a man or boy who has done something brave or good.
2 The **hero** of a story is the man or boy that it is about.

a
b
c
d
e
f
g
Hh
i
j
k
l
m
n
o
p
q
r
s
t
u
v
w
x
y
z

hexagon **hexagons**
A **hexagon** is a flat shape that has six sides.

hide **hides, hiding, hid, hidden**
1 If you **hide** something, you put it where no one can find it.
2 If you **hide**, you go where no one can see you.

high **higher, highest**
If something is **high**, it is tall or a long way from the ground.

hill **hills**
A **hill** is land that is higher than the land around it. A **hill** is not as tall as a mountain.

hip **hips**
Your **hip** is where your leg joins your body. (See page 174.)

hippopotamus
hippopotamuses or **hippopotami**
A **hippopotamus**, or **hippo** for short, is a very large African animal. It lives in or near a river.

his
His means belonging to a boy or a man.
*Dan can't find **his** books.*

history
Things that happened in the past are **history**.
*We learned about the Romans in our **history** lesson.*

hit **hits, hitting, hit**
If you **hit** something, you touch it very hard.
*The ball **hit** me so hard that I fell over.*

hive **hives**
When people keep bees, the bees live in a **hive**.

hold **holds, holding, held**
1 You **hold** something by taking it in your hand.
*My friend asked me if I would like to **hold** his pet hamster.*
2 A container **holds** the amount you can fit inside it.
*This jar **holds** 50 cookies.*

hole **holes**
A **hole** is an opening or empty space in something.
*There is a **hole** in my sweater.*

holiday holidays
If there is a **holiday**, you do not have to go to school or work.
Memorial Day is a holiday.

hollow
Something **hollow** has space inside it.
*Owls sometimes build their nests in **hollow** trees.*

home homes
Your **home** is the place where you live.
*My **home** is near the school.*

honest
If you are **honest**, you tell the truth and people trust you.

honey
Honey is a sweet, sticky food made by bees.

hoof hoofs or hooves
A **hoof** is the hard, bony part of a horse's foot. Cows, sheep and goats have **hooves**, too.

hop hops, hopping, hopped
1 When you **hop**, you jump on one foot. When birds **hop**, they jump with both feet together.
2 A **hop** is a small jump.

hope hopes, hoping, hoped
When you **hope** that something will happen, you want it to happen.
*I **hope** I pass the test!*

horn horns
A **horn** is the hard point that sticks out from the heads of some animals.

horrible
If you think something is **horrible**, you do not like it at all.
*Today's dessert was **horrible**!*

horse horses
A **horse** is a large animal that people ride. Some **horses** pull things, and some take part in races.

hospital hospitals
A **hospital** is a large building where sick people are looked after.

hot hotter, hottest
Something **hot** is very warm. Very **hot** things can burn you.
*Be careful! The water is very **hot**.*

a b c d e f g Hh i j k l m n o p q r s t u v w x y z

a
b
c
d
e
f
g
Hh
i
j
k
l
m
n
o
p
q
r
s
t
u
v
w
x
y
z

hotel   hotels
You can stay in a **hotel** when you are away from home. A **hotel** has lots of bedrooms.

hour   hours
An **hour** is made up of 60 minutes. There are 24 **hours** in a day.

house   houses
A **house** is a building that people live in. It has several rooms.

how
When you say **how** something happens, you explain the way that it happens.

huge
If something is **huge**, it is very, very big.
An elephant is a huge animal.

human   humans
A **human** is a person.

hump   humps
A **hump** is a big bump. Camels have **humps**.

hundred   hundreds
A **hundred** is the number 100. The number 342 has 3 **hundreds**, 4 tens, and 2 units.

hung   See **hang**.

hungry   hungrier, hungriest
When you are **hungry**, you want something to eat.
I'm hungry! I haven't eaten for hours.

hunt   hunts, hunting, hunted
1 When an animal **hunts**, it chases and kills another animal.
Owls hunt for mice at night.
2 When you **hunt** for something, you look everywhere for it.
I'm hunting for my socks.

hurry   hurries, hurrying, hurried
If you **hurry**, you move or do something quickly.
We were late, so we hurried to school.

hurt   hurts, hurting, hurt
If something **hurts**, you feel pain there.
My arm hurts where I banged it.

husband   husbands
A **husband** is a married man.

hut   huts
A **hut** is a small building. It is usually made of wood.

hutch   hutches
A **hutch** is a kind of cage made from wood and metal. Pet rabbits live in **hutches**.

ice

Ice is water that has frozen hard.
*Would you like some **ice** in your drink?*

ice cream   ice creams

Ice cream is a sweet, frozen food. It tastes creamy and comes in lots of flavors.

icicle   icicles

An **icicle** is a pointed, hanging piece of ice. It is made when dripping water freezes.
Icicles were hanging from the roof.

idea   ideas

An **idea** is something you have thought of yourself.
*I had a brilliant **idea**!*

igloo   igloos

An **igloo** is a kind of house. It is made from blocks of hard snow or ice.

ill

When you are **ill**, you do not feel very well.
*Kyle was **ill**, so he spent the day in bed.*

illness   illnesses

If you have an **illness**, you do not feel well. Colds and flu are **illnesses**.

illustration   illustrations

An **illustration** is a picture in a book.

illustrator   illustrators

An **illustrator** is someone who draws the pictures in a book.

imagine   imagines, imagining, imagined

If you **imagine** something, you picture it in your mind.

immediately

If something happens **immediately**, it happens right away.
*Stop that noise **immediately**!*

important

1 If something is **important**, it matters a lot.
*Good health is **important**.*
2 An **important** person has a lot of power.
*A president is an **important** person.*

a
b
c
d
e
f
g
h
Ii
j
k
l
m
n
o
p
q
r
s
t
u
v
w
x
y
z

impossible

If something is **impossible**, it cannot be done.

*It is **impossible** to walk on water.*

in

1 If someone or something is **in** a place, they are there.

*The shirts are **in** the drawer.*

2 If you are **in**, you are at home.

inch   inches

In the United States, **inches** are used to measure length.

index   indexes

An **index** is an alphabetical list at the back of a book. It tells you where to find things in the book.

Index

ant	3,10	hedgehog	15
anteater	4,8	hyena	17
antelope	5	lion	8
bear	7,18	monkey	21
camel	9	otter	19
crocodile	10	owl	5
dolphin	6,13	snake	7,29
elephant	2	tortoise	19
flamingo	6	walrus	12
gazelle	25	zebra	32

information

Information about something or someone is the facts about them.

*Have you any **information** about hot-air balloons?*

initial   initials

An **initial** is the first letter of a word or name.

*Sam Brown's **initials** are S.B.*

ink   inks

Ink is a colored liquid. It is used for printing or writing.

insect   insects

An **insect** is a tiny animal with six legs. **Insects** usually have wings. Flies and ants are **insects**.

inside   insides

The **inside** of something is surrounded by the rest of it.

*Open the box and look **inside** it!*

instruction   instructions

Instructions are words or drawings that tell you what to do.

*I followed the **instructions** on the box.*

instrument   instruments

1 An **instrument** is a tool people use to do a job.

*The doctor used an **instrument** to look in my ear.*

2 You play a musical **instrument** to make music. Recorders and violins are musical **instruments**.

interesting

If something is **interesting**, you want to know more about it.
*The film was so **interesting** that we watched it again.*

internet

You can look things up on the **internet** using a computer.

interrupt **interrupts, interrupting, interrupted**

If you start talking when someone is speaking, you **interrupt** them.
*Don't **interrupt** – let Ellie finish what she is saying!*

invent **invents, inventing, invented**

If you **invent** something, you are the first person to think of it.
*Alexander Graham Bell **invented** the telephone.*

investigate **investigates, investigating, investigated**

If you **investigate** something, you try to find out all about it.
*We are **investigating** what happens when you mix different colors.*

invisible

If something is **invisible**, you cannot see it.
*The school was **invisible** from the road.*

invitation **invitations**

You get an **invitation** when someone asks you to a party.

invite **invites, inviting, invited**

If you **invite** people to a party, you ask them to come to it.

iron **irons**

1 Iron is a strong, hard, gray metal.
2 People use a hot **iron** to smooth clothes.

island **islands**

(*sounds like* eye-land) An **island** is a piece of land that has water all around it.

its

Its means belonging to it.
*My bike has lost **its** wheel.*

it's

It's is short for it is or it has.
***It's** an interesting book.*
***It's** stopped raining now.*

a
b
c
d
e
f
g
h
i
Jj
k
l
m
n
o
p
q
r
s
t
u
v
w
x
y
z

jacket   jackets
A **jacket** is a short coat.

jam   jams
1 Jam is a sweet food. It is made from fruit and sugar.
*I had strawberry **jam** on my toast.*
2 There is also a **jam** when it is so crowded that nothing can move.
*The car was stuck in a traffic **jam**.*

January
January is the first month of the year. It has 31 days.

jar   jars
A **jar** is a glass container with a wide top. It is used for storing food, such as jam.

jaw   jaws
Your **jaw** is one of the bones that hold your teeth.

jeans
Jeans are pants made from a strong cotton material. They are often blue. (See page 176.)

jelly   jellies
Jelly is a soft, sweet food that you spread over bread.

jet   jets
1 A **jet** is an airplane that can fly very fast and very high.
2 A **jet** is also a narrow stream of something.
*A **jet** of water shot out through the hole in the pipe.*

jewel   jewels
A **jewel** is a beautiful, shiny stone that costs a lot of money. Diamonds and emeralds are **jewels**.

jewelry
Rings, necklaces, and earrings are **jewelry**. **Jewelry** is often made of gold or silver, sometimes with jewels.

jigsaw   jigsaws
A **jigsaw** is a puzzle. You fit together shapes to make a picture.
*This **jigsaw** puzzle has 100 pieces.*

job   jobs
1 A **job** is something you have to do.
*It's my **job** to collect the books.*
2 A **job** is also work that you are paid to do.
*My mom has a **job** as a bus driver.*

join joins, joining, joined

1 When you **join** things, you put them together.

2 If you **join** a club, you become a member of it.

Sophie has joined the swimming club.

joint joints

A **joint** is a part of the body where two bones fit together.

Your finger joints are called knuckles.

joke jokes

A **joke** is something that you say to make people laugh.

journey journeys

If you go on a **journey**, you travel from one place to another.

jug jugs

A **jug** is a container for holding liquids. It has a handle and a lip for pouring.

juice juices

Juice is the liquid that can be squeezed out of fruit.

I drink orange juice at breakfast.

July

July is the seventh month of the year. It has 31 days.

jump jumps, jumping, jumped

You **jump** when you move yourself into the air.

Tim jumped off the wall.

June

June is the sixth month of the year. It has 30 days.

jungle jungles

A **jungle** is a thick forest in a hot country.

just

If something has **just** happened, it happened a very short time ago.

I just got to school a minute ago.

a b c d e f g h i **Jj** k l m n o p q r s t u v w x y z

a
b
c
d
e
f
g
h
i
j
Kk
l
m
n
o
p
q
r
s
t
u
v
w
x
y
z

kangaroo kangaroos
A **kangaroo** is a large Australian animal. It jumps on its strong back legs. Female **kangaroos** carry their babies in a pocket on their stomachs.

keep keeps, keeping, kept
1 If you **keep** something, you save it.
I'll keep the last candy for you.
2 If you **keep** something somewhere, you always put it there.
I keep all my books in the bookcase.

kennel kennels
A **kennel** is a shelter for a dog or cat to sleep in.

kept See **keep**.

ketchup
Ketchup is a cold sauce made from tomatoes.

kettle kettles
People boil water in a **kettle**.

key keys, keying, keyed
1 A **key** is a piece of metal with a special shape. It opens a lock.
2 You press the **keys** on a piano or a computer with your fingers.
3 If you **key** in information on a computer keyboard, you type it in.

keyboard keyboards
A **keyboard** is all the keys on a computer or piano.

kick kicks, kicking, kicked
If you **kick** something, you hit it hard with your foot.
Malik kicked the ball into the air.

kid kids
1 A **kid** is a young goat.
2 Children are often called **kids**.

kill kills, killing, killed
If somebody **kills** something, he or she makes it die.
The fox killed the chicken.

kilogram or kilo
kilograms or kilos
You can measure mass in **kilograms** or **kilos**. A **kilogram** (kg) is 1000 grams (g).

kilometer kilometers
You can measure distance in **kilometers**. A **kilometer** (km) is 1000 meters (m).

kind kinder, kindest; kinds
1 A **kind** person is caring and helpful.
It was kind of Harry to lend me his bike.
2 Things of the same **kind** are part of the same group.
Cars and bikes are kinds of vehicles.

king kings
A **king** is a man who rules a country because he belongs to a royal family.

kingdom **kingdoms**
A **kingdom** is the area that is ruled by a king or queen.

kiss **kisses, kissing, kissed**
When you **kiss** someone, you touch them with your lips.
*Mom **kissed** me on the cheek.*

kitchen **kitchens**
A **kitchen** is a room where food is cooked.

kite **kites**
A **kite** is a toy that you fly in the air. It is tied to a long piece of string.

kitten **kittens**
A **kitten** is a young cat.

knee **knees**
Your **knee** is the part of your leg that bends. (See page 174.)

kneel **kneels, kneeling**
knelt or kneeled
When you **kneel**, you get down on your knees.

knew See **know**.

knife **knives**
A **knife** is a tool for cutting things. It has a handle and a sharp blade.

knight **knights**
Hundreds of years ago, a **knight** was a soldier who wore armor and rode a horse.

knit **knits, knitting, knitted**
When you **knit**, you make clothes using wool and a pair of long needles.

knives See **knife**.

knock **knocks, knocking, knocked**
1 If you **knock** something, you hit it hard.
2 If you **knock** on a door, you make a noise to tell people you are there.

knot **knots**
A **knot** is made by tying two pieces of string together.

know **knows, knowing, knew, known**
1 If you **know** something, it is in your mind and you do not need to learn it.
2 If you **know** someone, you have met them before.

koala **koalas**
A **koala** is a small Australian animal.

label **labels**
A **label** is
a small tag
that tells you
more about
something.

lace **laces**
1 Lace is a kind of pretty cloth with
lots of holes in it.
2 Lace is also another word for
shoelace.

ladder **ladders**
You climb up a **ladder**
to reach something high.
Ladders are made
of metal or wood.

lady **ladies**
Lady is a polite word for a woman.

ladybug **ladybugs**
A **ladybug** is a small
red beetle with
black spots. It is
often found
in gardens.

laid See **lay**.

lain See **lie²**.

lake **lakes**
A **lake** is a large area of fresh water
with land all around it.

lamb **lambs**
A **lamb** is a
young sheep.

lamp **lamps**
You turn on a
lamp to give
you light when
it is dark.

land **lands, landing, landed**
1 When you **land** somewhere, you
arrive after a journey by airplane.
We landed at the airport.
2 Land is the dry part of the Earth
not covered by water.

lane **lanes**
A **lane** is a narrow road.

language **languages**
Language is the words people use
to speak and write. People in
different countries speak different
languages.

lap **laps, lapping, lapped**
1 When you sit down, the tops of
your legs make your **lap**.
The cat likes to sit on my lap.
2 An animal **laps** when it drinks
using its tongue.
The cat lapped up its milk.

large **larger, largest**
If something is **large**, it is big.
Katie and I shared a large drink.

last **lasts, lasting, lasted**
1 When something is **last**, it comes at the end.
The last month of the year is December.
2 If something **lasts**, it goes on for some time.
This film lasts an hour.

late **later, latest**
1 If you are **late**, you arrive after you are expected.
2 The **late** part of something is near the end.
We'll get there by late afternoon.

laugh **laughs, laughing, laughed**
When you **laugh**, you make a sound to show that something is funny.
We all laughed at the clown.

law **laws**
A **law** is a rule that everyone in a country must follow.
Dropping litter is against the law.

lawn **lawns**
A **lawn** is the grass that grows next to a house.

lay **lays, laying, laid**
1 If you **lay** something down, you put it down carefully.
Please lay your pencils down on the table.
2 If you **lay** the table, you get it ready for a meal.
3 When a hen **lays** an egg, it pushes it out of its body.
See **lie²**.

layer **layers**
A **layer** is something flat that goes above or below something else.
Mom covered the carpet with a layer of newspaper.

lazy **lazier, laziest**
A **lazy** person does not want to work.
I feel too lazy to get out of bed!

lead **leads, leading, led**
1 (*sounds like* seed) If you **lead** someone, you go in front of them to show the way.
You lead and we'll follow.
2 (*sounds like* seed) If you **lead** in a race, you are in front of the other runners.
Joe was leading the others until the last few feet.
3 (*sounds like* seed) A **lead** is a long piece of leather that you fix to a dog's collar.
4 (*sounds like* red) **Lead** is a heavy, soft, gray metal.
5 (*sounds like* red) The **lead** of a pencil is the part that makes marks.

leader **leaders**
The **leader** of a group is in charge of it.
The captain is the leader of the team.

a
b
c
d
e
f
g
h
i
j
k

Ll

m
n
o
p
q
r
s
t
u
v
w
x
y
z

leaf leaves
A **leaf** is a flat, green part of a tree or plant. **Leaves** grow out of branches or stems.

lean leans, leaning, leaned
If you **lean**, you bend in one direction.
That tree leans over the road.

leap leaps, leaping, leapt or leaped
1 If you **leap**, you jump a long way.
Megan leapt across the stream.
2 In a **leap year**, February has 29 days instead of 28.

learn learns, learning, learned
When you **learn** something, you get to know something new.
I am learning to ride a bike.

least
Least means the smallest amount.
Sarah and Ian ate most of the popcorn – I had the least.

leather
Leather is made from the skin of animals. Shoes and bags can be made of **leather**.

leave leaves, leaving, left
1 When you **leave** a place, you go away from it.
2 If you **leave** something somewhere, you do not take it with you.

leaves See **leaf** and **leave**.

led See **lead**.

left
Left is the opposite of right. When you read or write, you start at the **left** side of the page.
Tom has his left foot on the ball.

leg legs
Your **legs** are parts of your body.
(See page 174.)

lemon lemons
A **lemon** is a small yellow fruit. It has a very sharp flavor.

lemonade
Lemonade is a cold drink that is made from lemons, sugar, and water.

lend lends, lending, lent
When someone **lends** you something, they give it to you for a short time. Then you give it back.
Please, will you lend me your pencil sharpener?

length lengths
You measure how long something is to find out its **length**.

lent See **lend**.

less

Less means not as much.
*If you have a large drink and I have a small drink, I have **less** than you.*

lesson lessons

A **lesson** is a time when you are taught something.
*I had a swimming **lesson** today.*

let lets, letting, let

If someone **lets** you do something, they say you may do it.
*Nicky **let** me ride her bicycle.*

letter letters

1 A **letter** is a written message.
*I wrote a **letter** to my grandma in Australia.*
2 A **letter** is one of the symbols you use to write words.
*A, B, C, D are capital **letters** and a, b, c, d are lowercase **letters**.*

lettuce lettuces

Lettuce is a green vegetable. Its leaves are often used in salads.

level

If something is **level**, it is flat.
*A table needs to be **level**.*

library libraries

A **library** is a place where lots of books are kept. You can borrow books from a **library** to read at home.

lick licks, licking, licked

If you **lick** something, you move your tongue across it.
*The dog **licked** the bowl clean.*

lid lids

A **lid** is a cover on a container. You take off the **lid** to open the container.
*Tim took the **lid** off the pan.*

lie¹ lies, lying, lied

If you **lie** or tell a **lie**, you say something that you know is not true.

lie² lies, lying, lay, lain

If you **lie** down, you rest your body flat on something.
*Our cat **lies** in the sun all day.*

life lives

Your **life** is the time when you are alive. The **life** of a person or animal begins when they are born and ends when they die.

lifeboat lifeboats

A **lifeboat** is a boat that goes to save people who are in danger at sea.

lift lifts, lifting, lifted

1 If you **lift** something, you pick it up and move it upward.
*I'll **lift** that heavy box for you.*
2 A **lift** in a garage raises cars so they can be fixed.

a
b
c
d
e
f
g
h
i
j
k
Ll
m
n
o
p
q
r
s
t
u
v
w
x
y
z

a
b
c
d
e
f
g
h
i
j
k
Ll
m
n
o
p
q
r
s
t
u
v
w
x
y
z

light **lights, lighting, lit; lighter, lightest**
1 Light comes from the sun during the day.
2 A **light** is a lamp that you turn on to help you see when it is dark.
3 If you **light** something, you make it start to burn.
4 Something **light** is not heavy.
5 A **light** color is pale.

lighthouse **lighthouses**
A **lighthouse** is a tower with a bright, flashing light at the top. It warns ships of dangerous rocks.

lightning
Lightning is a very bright flash of light in the sky during a thunderstorm.

like **likes, liking, liked**
1 If you **like** someone, you think they are very nice.
2 If one thing is **like** another, it is the same in some way.
*Sam's bike is **like** mine.*

likely **likelier, likeliest**
Something that is **likely** will probably happen.
*Susie works hard, so she's **likely** to do well.*

line **lines**
1 A **line** is a long, thin mark. **Lines** can be straight or curved.
*Put a **line** under the date.*
2 A **line** is also a row of people or things.
*We wait in a **line** for our dinner.*
3 When you make a **line** with other people, you are waiting for something.
*There was a **line** outside the movie house.*

lion **lions**
A **lion** is a large wild cat. It eats other animals.

lip **lips**
Your **lips** are the parts of your face around your mouth. (See page 174.)

liquid **liquids**
A **liquid** is something that pours easily and is not solid. Water, milk, oil, and fruit juice are all **liquids**.

list **lists**
If you make a **list**, you write things down one after another.
*Mom wrote the things she needed on a shopping **list**.*

listen **listens, listening, listened**
When you **listen**, you try to hear something.

lit See **light**.

liter liters
You can measure liquid in **liters**.
A **liter** (l) is 1000 milliliters (ml).
Can I have a liter of milk, please?

litter
Litter is garbage that people drop
on the ground.
Please take your litter home with you.

little less, least
1 If something is **little**, it is small.
*Grandpa gave some milk to the little
kitten.*
2 A **little** means only a small
amount.
Grandpa only gave the kitten a little milk.

live lives, living, lived
1 If you **live,** you are alive and
breathing.
2 If you **live** in a place, your home is
there.
David lives in New York.

lives See **life** and **live.**

lizard lizards
A **lizard** is a reptile with four legs
and a long tail. **Lizards** have rough,
dry skins.

load loads, loading, loaded
When you **load** a vehicle, you put
lots of things on it or in it.
We loaded the car with suitcases.

loaf loaves
You can cut a **loaf** of bread into
slices. Some **loaves** are already
sliced.

local
If something is **local**, it is near to
your home.
I go to the local school.

lock locks, locking, locked
1 If something is **locked**, you need
a key to open it.
2 A **lock** keeps a door or suitcase
shut. It can only be opened with the
right key.

locomotive locomotives
A **locomotive** is a huge machine
with iron wheels that runs over a
road made of rails.
*This locomotive can pull 80 freight
cars.*

lodge lodges
A **lodge** is a house or an inn where
people spend their vacation.

log logs
A **log** is a large piece of wood from
a tree.

lollipop lollipops
A **lollipop** is candy on a stick. It is
also called a lolly.

lonely lonelier, loneliest
If you are **lonely**, you are unhappy
because you are alone.
*My grandma gets lonely, so I often go
to see her.*

a
b
c
d
e
f
g
h
i
j
k
Ll
m
n
o
p
q
r
s
t
u
v
w
x
y
z

long **longer, longest**
1 Something **long** is a great distance from end to end.
2 A **long** time is a great amount of time. **Long** ago means many years ago.

look **looks, looking, looked**
1 If you **look** at something, you turn your eyes toward it so you can see it.
*I **looked** at my dirty hands.*
2 If you **look** for something, you try to find it.
*Peter **looked** everywhere for his coat.*

loose **looser, loosest**
Something that is **loose** moves around.
*Sasha has a **loose** tooth.*

lose **loses, losing, lost**
1 If you **lose** something, you cannot find it.
*I've **lost** my book. I don't know where it is!*
2 If you **lose** a race, you do not come in first.

lost
If you are **lost**, you do not know where you are.
*We were **lost**, so we asked the way.*
See **lose**.

lot **lots**
A **lot** means a large number or amount.
*There are a **lot** of boys in my class.*

loud **louder, loudest**
Something **loud** is very noisy.
*The music got **louder** as the band came up the road.*

love **loves, loving, loved**
1 Love is a very strong feeling of liking for someone.
2 If you **love** someone, you like them very, very much.

lovely **lovelier, loveliest**
Something **lovely** is very nice to see, hear, smell, or do.
*That music is **lovely**!*
*I had a **lovely** birthday.*

low **lower, lowest**
Something **low** is not very high.

lucky **luckier, luckiest**
If you are **lucky**, good things seem to happen to you.
*I'm really **lucky** – I've got a new bike!*

lump **lumps**
A **lump** is a solid piece of something.
*Mom put a **lump** of sugar in her coffee.*

lunch **lunches**
Lunch is the meal that you eat in the middle of the day.

lying See **lie**.

Mm

machine machines
A **machine** makes things or does a job. **Machines** often use electricity.
Our dirty clothes go into the washing machine.

made See **make**.

magazine magazines
A **magazine** is a thin book with lots of pictures. It usually comes out once a week or once a month.

magic
In fairy tales, **magic** things happen that could not happen in real life.
Cinderella's rags turned into a beautiful dress by magic!

magician magicians
A **magician** does clever tricks that seem impossible.
The magician pulled a rabbit out of an empty hat.

magnet magnets
A **magnet** is a special piece of metal that some metal things stick to.

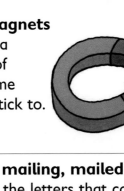

mail mails, mailing, mailed
1 The **mail** is the letters that come to your house.

2 When you **mail** a letter, you put it in a mailbox.

mail carrier mail carriers
A **mail carrier** collects and delivers letters and parcels.

main
The **main** thing is the most important one.
The bank is on the main street.

make makes, making, made
1 When you **make** something, you put things together until you have something new.
We made a clubhouse out of boxes.
2 If you are **made** to do something, somebody sees that you do it.
My mom made me put my coat on.

a b c d e f g h i j k l

Mm

n o p q r s t u v w x y z

a
b
c
d
e
f
g
h
i
j
k
l

Mm

n
o
p
q
r
s
t
u
v
w
x
y
z

male males
A **male** person or animal can be a father. Boys and men are **males**.

mammal mammals
A **mammal** is an animal that feeds its babies with its own milk. People, whales, and cats are all **mammals**.

man men
A **man** is a grown-up male person.

manage manages, managing, managed
When you **manage** to do something, you are able to do something difficult.

many
Many means a lot of.
*There are **many** words in this dictionary.*

map maps
A **map** is a drawing that helps you find your way around.

March
March is the third month of the year. It has 31 days.

mark marks, marking, marked
1 A **mark** is a spot or scratch that spoils something.
2 You **mark** something to know that it is yours.
3 Your teacher **marks** your work to say whether it is right or wrong.

market markets
A **market** is a place where people buy and sell things.

marmalade
Marmalade is a kind of jam, usually made from oranges.

married
A **married** person has a husband or a wife.

marry marries, marrying, married
When two people **marry**, they become each other's husband and wife.

mask masks
You wear a **mask** over your face to make you look different.

mass
The **mass** of something is how much there is or how heavy it is.

mat mats

A **mat** is a thick piece of material. It protects a surface or makes it softer.

match matches, matching, matched

1 A **match** is a game between two teams.

2 A **match** is a little stick that people use to light a fire.

3 If you put similar things together, you **match** them.

material materials

1 Material is the stuff that things are made of. Metal, glass, wood, and plastic are **materials**.

2 Material is also the cloth that is used to make things like clothes.

matter matters, mattered

If something **matters**, it is important.

mattress mattresses

A **mattress** is the thick, soft part of a bed that you sleep on.

may

1 If something **may** happen, it is possible that it will happen.

2 If someone says you **may** do something, you are allowed to do it.

May

May is the fifth month of the year. It has 31 days.

meal meals

You have a **meal** when you sit down and eat. Breakfast and dinner are both **meals**.

mean means, meaning, meant; meaner, meanest

1 If you know what something **means**, you are able to explain it.
A dictionary explains what words mean.

2 If you **mean** to do something, you plan to do it.
I didn't mean to push you.

3 A **mean** person is unkind and selfish.
Don't be mean – share it with Ed!

meanwhile

Meanwhile means while something else is happening.

measles

If you have **measles**, you have a fever and lots of red spots.

measure measures, measuring, measured

1 If you **measure** something, you find out its size. (See page 183.)

2 A **measure** is something you use when you **measure**, like a ruler or a jug.

meat

Meat is food that comes from part of an animal.

medicine medicines

When you are ill, you take **medicine** to make you better.

a
b
c
d
e
f
g
h
i
j
k
l
Mm
n
o
p
q
r
s
t
u
v
w
x
y
z

a
b
c
d
e
f
g
h
i
j
k
l

Mm

n
o
p
q
r
s
t
u
v
w
x
y
z

medium
Medium means neither large nor small.

meet   meets, meeting, met
If you **meet** someone, you are in the same place at the same time.
*We will **meet** Sue at the station at noon.*

melon   melons
A **melon** is a large, round, juicy fruit. It has yellow or green skin.

melt   melts, melting, melted
When a solid **melts**, it changes into a liquid because it has been heated.
*The sun **melted** my ice cream.*

memory   memories
You use your **memory** when you remember things.
*You learned that quickly – you have a good **memory**!*

men   See **man**.

mend   mends, mending, mended
If you **mend** something that is torn, you sew it.
*When I tore my blouse, mom **mended** it.*

mental
Something **mental** is done in your head.
*When you do **mental** math, you work out the answer in your head.*

menu   menus
1 A **menu** in a restaurant is a list of what you can order to eat.
2 A **menu** on a computer screen is a list of things you can choose from.

mess
Things in a **mess** are untidy.

message   messages
You send or leave a **message** when you cannot speak to someone yourself.
*Dad left a **message** to say he'll be early.*

messy   messier, messiest
If something is **messy**, it is dirty or untidy.

met   See **meet**.

metal   metals
Metal is a hard, cold material. Steel is a **metal** used to make cars. Gold is a **metal** used to make jewelry.

meter   meters
You can measure length in **meters**. There are 100 centimeters (cm) in a **meter** (m).
*John is 1 **meter** 50 centimeters tall.*

method   methods
A **method** is a way of doing something.

metropolis   metropolises
A very large and important city is a **metropolis**.

mice See **mouse**.

microwave **microwaves**
A **microwave** oven cooks food very quickly.

middle **middles**
The **middle** of something is between its edges or ends.
The cat is in the middle of the rug.

midnight
Midnight means 12 o'clock at night.

might
If something **might** happen, it is possible that it will.

mile **miles**
A **mile** is a way to measure distance. A **mile** is longer than a kilometer.

milk
Milk is a white liquid. Female mammals make **milk** in their bodies to feed their babies. The **milk** that you drink comes from cows.

millennium **millennia**
A **millennium** is 1000 years.

milliliter **milliliters**
You can measure liquid in **milliliters**. There are 1000 **milliliters** (ml) in a liter (l).

millimeter **millimeters**
You can measure length in **millimeters**. There are 10 **millimeters** (mm) in a centimeter (cm), and 1000 **millimeters** in a meter (m).

10 mm   20 mm   30 mm   40 mm   50 mm

mind **minds, minding, minded**
1 Your **mind** is your thoughts and memories.
2 If you **mind** about something, you care about it.
3 If you **mind** something for someone, you look after it.
John is minding the store.

mine
Mine means belonging to me.
That pen is yours and this pen is mine.

minus
Minus is another word you can use when you take away or subtract. The symbol – means **minus**.

minute **minutes**
A **minute** is made up of 60 seconds. There are 60 **minutes** in an hour.

mirror **mirrors**
A **mirror** is a special piece of glass. When you look in a **mirror**, you see yourself.

a b c d e f g h i j k l **Mm** n o p q r s t u v w x y z

a
b
c
d
e
f
g
h
i
j
k
l

Mm

n
o
p
q
r
s
t
u
v
w
x
y
z

miss misses, missing, missed

1 If you **miss** a bus or train, you arrive too late to catch it.

2 If you try to hit something and **miss**, you do not hit it.

3 If you **miss** someone, you feel sad because they are not with you.

Miss

Miss can be used before the name of a girl or unmarried woman.

missing

If something is **missing**, it is lost.

mistake mistakes

A **mistake** is something that is wrong.

*Well done! You have made no **mistakes**.*

mix mixes, mixing, mixed

When you **mix** things, you put them together to make something new.

Mix blue and yellow paint to make green.

mixture mixtures

A **mixture** is a number of different things put together.

*This green paint is a **mixture** of blue and yellow.*

mobile phone mobile phones

A **mobile phone** is a telephone that people can carry.

model models

A **model** is a small copy of something. It shows what it looks like or how it works.

*Dan's building a **model** airplane.*

modern

If something is **modern**, it is new and uses the latest ideas and equipment.

mole moles

1 A **mole** is a small, furry animal with tiny eyes. It lives under the ground.

2 A **mole** is also a small, dark spot on someone's skin.

mom or mommy moms or mommies

Mom or **mommy** is what you call your mother.

moment moments

A **moment** is a very short time.

*Jenny stopped for a **moment** to pull up her socks.*

Monday Mondays

Monday is the day of the week between Sunday and Tuesday.

money

Money is the bills and coins you use to pay for things.

monkey monkeys

A **monkey** is a small animal with a long tail. **Monkeys** live in hot countries and can climb trees.

monster monsters

In stories, a **monster** is a huge, frightening creature.

month **months**
A **month** has 28 to 31 days. There are 12 **months** in a year.

moon **moons**
You see the **moon** shining in the sky at night. The **moon** moves around the Earth once every four weeks.

mop **mops**
A **mop** is a long handle with strips of cloth joined to the end. You use a **mop** to wash the floor.

more
If someone has **more** than you, they have a larger number or amount than you have.

morning **mornings**
Morning is the first part of the day. You get up in the **morning**.

mosque **mosques**
A **mosque** is a building where some people go to pray.

most
The person who has **most** has more than anyone else.
*Richard has more books than me, but Hirani has the **most**.*

moth **moths**
A **moth** is an insect that looks like a butterfly. It usually flies around at night.

mother **mothers**
A **mother** is a woman who has had a child.

motorcycle **motorcycles**
A **motorcycle** is a vehicle with two wheels and an engine.

mountain **mountains**
A **mountain** is a very high hill. It is very steep and difficult to climb.
*Mount Everest is the highest **mountain** in the world.*

mouse **mice**
1 A **mouse** is a small animal with a long tail and sharp teeth.
2 You use a **mouse** to control the cursor on a computer screen.

mouth **mouths**
You eat and speak with your **mouth**. It is part of your face. (See page 174.)

a b c d e f g h i j k l

Mm

n o p q r s t u v w x y z

95

a
b
c
d
e
f
g
h
i
j
k
l

Mm

n
o
p
q
r
s
t
u
v
w
x
y
z

move moves, moving, moved
If you **move**, you go to a different place or position.

movement movements
When a person or thing moves, it makes a **movement**.

mud
Mud is a wet and sticky mixture of earth and water.

muddy muddier, muddiest
If something is **muddy**, it is covered with wet earth.
Take off those muddy shoes!

multiple multiples
When you multiply a number, you get a **multiple** of it.
6, 9, and 12 are all multiples of 3.

multiplication
Multiplication is a quick way to add together lots of groups of the same number. The symbol × is for **multiplication**.

multiply multiplies, multiplying, multiplied
You **multiply** when you do multiplication.
2 multiplied by 3 is 6.

$2 \times 3 = 6$ or $2 + 2 + 2 = 6$

munch munches, munching, munched
If you **munch**, you chew noisily.

muscle muscles
Muscles are the parts inside your body that you use when you move.
You can feel a muscle in your arm when you bend it.

museum museums
You go to a **museum** to see lots of interesting things.
I saw a rocket at the Science Museum.

mushroom mushrooms
A **mushroom** is a plant with no leaves. You sometimes find **mushrooms** growing among grass.

music
Music is sounds made by people singing or playing instruments like pianos and recorders.

must
If someone **must** do something, they have to do it.
You must look before you cross the road!

nail **nails**
1 Your **nails** are the hard parts at the ends of your fingers and toes.
2 A **nail** is a piece of metal with a pointed end. It is used to join two pieces of wood together.

name **names**
A **name** is what you call a person, place, or thing.
*My **name** is Josie.*
*The **name** of Ireland's capital city is Dublin.*

narrow **narrower, narrowest**
Something that is **narrow** measures very little between one side and the other.

nasty **nastier, nastiest**
Something **nasty** is not nice.

natural
Something that is **natural** is not made by people or machines.
*Wood and cotton are **natural** materials, but plastic is not.*

nature
Nature is everything in the world that is not made by people. Wild animals, mountains, and the weather are part of **nature**.

naughty **naughtier, naughtiest**
A **naughty** child behaves badly.

near **nearer, nearest**
Something **near** is not far away.

nearly
Nearly means not quite.
*Tara's **nearly** old enough to go to school.*
*Harry **nearly** fell over.*

neat **neater, neatest**
If something is **neat**, it is tidy.
*Callum has folded his clothes into a **neat** pile.*

neck **necks**
Your **neck** joins your head to the rest of your body. (See page 174.)

necklace **necklaces**
A **necklace** is a piece of jewelry that is worn around the neck.

need **needs, needing, needed**
If you **need** something, you must have it.
*I **need** a bag to carry my books.*

needle **needles**
A **needle** is a thin piece of metal with a point. **Needles** are used for sewing. Special **needles** are used for knitting.

a
b
c
d
e
f
g
h
i
j
k
l
m
Nn
o
p
q
r
s
t
u
v
w
x
y
z

97

a
b
c
d
e
f
g
h
i
j
k
l
m
Nn
o
p
q
r
s
t
u
v
w
x
y
z

neighbor   neighbors
A **neighbor** is someone who lives very near you.

nephew   nephews
A person's **nephew** is the son of his or her brother or sister.

nervous
If you are **nervous**, you feel worried or afraid.

nest   nests
A **nest** is the home that some animals make for their young ones.

net   nets
1 Net is a material with lots of holes. It is made of knotted thread or string.
2 A **net** is used to catch fish, or in some games like tennis and soccer.
The ball shot into the back of the net.

nettle   nettles
A **nettle** is a wild plant. It has rough leaves that sting.

never
If something **never** happens, it does not happen at any time.
Greg never gets to school on time.

new   newer, newest
1 Something **new** has not been used before.
2 New also means different.
We did something new today – we played badminton.

news
News is information about things that have just happened.
I've got some exciting news! I won my race!

newspaper   newspapers
A **newspaper** tells you in words and pictures what has happened in the world.

next
1 Next means the one nearest to you.
I spoke to the girl at the next table.
2 Next also means the one that comes after this one.
I'll see you next week.

nice   nicer, nicest
If something or someone is **nice**, you like it or him.

niece   nieces
A person's **niece** is the daughter of his or her brother or sister.

night   nights
Night is the time when it is dark and most people sleep.
Did you see the stars last night?

nightgown nightgowns

A **nightgown** is a loose dress that girls and women wear in bed. (See page 176.)

nightmare nightmares

A **nightmare** is a frightening dream.

no

1 If you say **no**, you do not agree with someone or you will not do something.

2 No also means none at all.

*My uncle has **no** children.*

nobody

Nobody means no person or no one.

*I opened the door but **nobody** was there.*

nod nods, nodding, nodded

When you **nod**, you move your head up and down quickly.

noise noises

Noise is the sounds that someone or something makes.

*The **noise** of the storm kept me awake.*

noisy noisier, noisiest

Something **noisy** makes a lot of noise.

none

None means not one.

*Sunil has 12 pencils but I have **none**.*

nonfiction

Nonfiction books tell you about real people and things.

nonsense

If someone talks **nonsense**, what they say does not mean anything.

noon

Noon means 12 o'clock in the middle of the day.

no one

No one means not one person or nobody.

*I opened the door but **no one** was there.*

north

North is a direction. It is on your left when you look toward the rising sun in the morning.

nose noses

Your **nose** is part of your face. You breathe and smell through your **nose**. (See page 174.)

nostril nostrils

Your **nostrils** are the two holes in your nose that you breathe through.

a b c d e f g h i j k l m **Nn** o p q r s t u v w x y z

a
b
c
d
e
f
g
h
i
j
k
l
m
Nn
o
p
q
r
s
t
u
v
w
x
y
z

note notes
1 A **note** is a short letter.
2 You make **notes** to help you remember something.
3 You **note** something when you observe it carefully.
4 A **note** can also be a single sound in music.

nothing
If you do not have anything, you have **nothing**.

notice notices, noticing, noticed
1 If you **notice** something, you see it and start to think about it.
2 A **notice** is a sign that tells people something.
*The **notice** said: "Keep off the grass."*

Keep off the grass

noun nouns
A **noun** is a word for a person, animal, place, or thing.

November
November is the eleventh month of the year. It has 30 days.

now
Now means at the present time.
*You are reading these words **now**.*

nowhere
Nowhere means not any place.
*We have **nowhere** to play football when the park is closed.*

number numbers
A **number** can be written using letters or symbols. You use **numbers** to count things or people.
*You can see more **numbers** on page 183.*

3 three
four **4** ten **10**
seven **7**
six **6** two **2**

nurse nurses
A **nurse** looks after sick people.
Nurses usually work in hospitals.

nursery nurseries
1 A **nursery** is a place where young children go to play and learn.
2 A **nursery** school is a school for children up to five years of age.

nursery rhyme nursery rhymes
A **nursery rhyme** is a poem or song for young children.

nut nuts
A **nut** is a dry brown seed inside a hard shell. It grows on a tree.

Oo

oak oaks
An **oak** is a large tree. It has seeds called acorns. Its hard wood is often used to make furniture.

oar oars
An **oar** is a long pole with a flat end. You pull on an **oar** to move a boat through water.

oats
Oats are the seeds of a plant. They are used to make food for people and animals.

obey obeys, obeying, obeyed
When you **obey** someone, you do what they say.

ocean oceans
An **ocean** is a huge sea.

o'clock
You use **o'clock** when you say a time that is exactly on the hour.
Five o'clock means exactly five hours after noon or midnight.

octagon octagons
An **octagon** is a flat shape that has eight sides. (See page 184.)

October
October is the tenth month of the year. It has 31 days.

octopus octopuses
An **octopus** is a sea creature. It catches food with its eight long arms.

odd odder, oddest
1 An **odd** number cannot be divided exactly by two. There will always be one left over.
2 Something **odd** is a bit strange.

off
1 If you take **off** your coat, you do not wear it anymore.
2 If a light or machine is **off**, it is not switched on.
3 When you get **off** something, you are not on it anymore.
*We get **off** the bus at the next stop.*

offer offers, offering, offered
If you **offer** something to someone, you ask if he or she would like it.
*I **offered** Ronan some ice cream.*

office offices
An **office** is a room where people work.

often
Often means many times.
*We **often** have a picnic outside in the summer.*

a
b
c
d
e
f
g
h
i
j
k
l
m
n
Oo
p
q
r
s
t
u
v
w
x
y
z

oil oils
Oil is a smooth, thick liquid. One kind of **oil** is burned to keep people warm or used in machines. Another kind of **oil** is used for cooking food.

old older, oldest
An **old** person was born a long time ago. Something **old** was made a long time ago.

once
1 If something happens **once**, it happens one time only.
2 If something happens at **once**, it happens right away.

onion onions
An **onion** is a white or red vegetable with a strong taste.

only
Only means one or no more than.
*You can **only** have one chocolate.*
*Gary's little – he's **only** three.*
*This is the **only** box I can find.*

open opens, opening, opened
1 When something is **open**, it is no longer closed.
2 If you **open** something, you make it **open**.
*Dad **opened** the door.*

operation operations
When doctors repair a person's body, they do an **operation**.

opposite opposites
The **opposite** of something is different from it in every way.
*Light is the **opposite** of dark.*

orange oranges
1 An **orange** is a round, juicy fruit. It has a thick **orange** skin.

2 **Orange** is a color made from a mixture of red and yellow. (See page 184.)

orchestra orchestras
An **orchestra** is a large group of people who play musical instruments together.

order orders, ordering, ordered
1 The **order** of things is how they are arranged.
The words in this book are in alphabetical order.
2 If you **order** something in a restaurant, you say you would like it.
3 If you are **ordered** to do something, you must do it.

ordinary

Ordinary means not special in any way.

*It was a very **ordinary** day. Nothing different happened.*

other

Other means not this one.

*Take your bag in this hand and hold the rail with the **other**.*

otter   otters

An **otter** is a furry, long-tailed animal. It lives near water. **Otters** swim well and eat fish.

our

Our means belonging to us.

*This is **our** car.*

out

1 If you go **out**, you are away from home.

*We went **out** for a meal.*

2 If a light or fire goes **out**, it stops burning.

outside

1 The **outside** of something is the part around the rest of it.

2 If you are **outside**, you are not in a building.

oval   ovals

An **oval** is a flat shape with a curved edge. It is like the shape of an egg.

oven   ovens

An **oven** is the inside of a stove where you bake food.

over

When something is **over**, it is finished.

*When the game was **over**, we all went home.*

owe   owes, owing, owed

If you **owe** someone money, you have not paid them for something or you have not paid back what they lent you.

owl   owls

An **owl** is a bird that usually hunts at night. It has large eyes to help it to see in the dark.

own   owns, owning, owned

1 If you **own** something, it belongs to you.

2 If you are on your **own**, you are alone.

a
b
c
d
e
f
g
h
i
j
k
l
m
n
Oo
p
q
r
s
t
u
v
w
x
y
z

103

a
b
c
d
e
f
g
h
i
j
k
l
m
n
o

q
r
s
t
u
v
w
x
y
z

pack   packs, packing, packed
When you **pack** a case or container, you put things in it.
*Masud **packed** his bags and went on vacation.*

package   packages
A **package** is a closed container or a parcel that contains something inside.
*There were three books in the **package**.*

paddle   paddles, paddling, paddled
When you **paddle**, you walk in water that is not very deep.

page   pages
A **page** is one side of a piece of paper in a book, magazine, or newspaper.
*This is **page** 104 of this dictionary.*

paid   See **pay**.

pain   pains
You feel a **pain** when part of your body hurts.

paint   paints, painting, painted
1 Paint is a liquid that you use to change the color of something.
2 You can **paint** walls or pictures.

painting   paintings
A **painting** is a picture that someone has painted.

pair   pairs
1 Two things that go together make a **pair**. Shoes, feet, and eyes all come in **pairs**.
2 Something that has two similar parts joined together can also be a **pair**.
*I want a **pair** of shoes to go with this **pair** of pants.*

pajamas
Pajamas are a loose top and pants that you wear in bed.

palace   palaces
A **palace** is a very large house. Kings, queens, and other important people live in **palaces**.

pale   paler, palest
If a color is **pale**, it is almost white.

palm   palms
1 Your **palm** is the inside part of your hand. (See page 174.)

2 A **palm** tree grows in hot countries. It has large leaves but no branches.

pan pans
A **pan** is a round metal container with a long handle. It is used for cooking things on top of a stove.

pancake pancakes
A **pancake** is a very thin, flat cake. It is cooked in a flat pan.

panda pandas
A **panda** is an animal that looks like a bear and lives in China. The one in the photo is a giant panda

panic panics, panicking, panicked
1 Panic is a sudden feeling of fear.
2 If you **panic**, you feel so afraid that you cannot think properly.

pantomime pantomimes
A **pantomime** is a kind of play that requires you to tell a story without speaking: all you can do is make faces and move your body.

pants
You wear **pants** to cover your body from your waist to your ankles. **Pants** have separate legs.

panty panties
Panties are underpants worn by women and girls. (See page 176.)

paper papers
1 Paper is a thin material. You write on **paper** and wrap parcels with it. Books are printed on **paper**.
2 Paper is also short for newspaper.

parcel parcels
You wrap something in a **parcel** to send it in the mail or give it as a present.

parent parents
Your **parents** are your mother and your father.

park parks, parking, parked
1 A **park** is a large open space with grass and trees. People walk and play in **parks**.
2 When someone **parks** a car, they leave it for a short time.

a
b
c
d
e
f
g
h
i
j
k
l
m
n
o

Pp

q
r
s
t
u
v
w
x
y
z

parrot parrots

A **parrot** is a brightly colored bird with a curved beak. Some **parrots** copy human speech.

part parts

A **part** is anything that belongs to something bigger.
*Your eyes, nose, and mouth are **parts** of your face.*

party parties

A **party** is a group of people having fun together.

pass passes, passing, passed

1 When you **pass** something, you go by it without stopping.
2 When you **pass** something to someone, you give it to them.
3 If you **pass** a test, you do well.

passenger passengers

A **passenger** travels in a car, bus, train, airplane, or ship.

passport passports

A **passport** is a small book that you carry when you travel to another country.

past

The **past** is the time before now.
*One minute ago, ten years ago, and thousands of years ago are all in the **past**.*

pasta

Pasta is a food that you eat with sauce. Spaghetti, macaroni, and noodles are all different types of **pasta**.

paste pastes, pasting, pasted

1 **Paste** is a kind of glue. It is used for sticking paper onto things.
2 If you **paste** something, you stick it with glue or **paste**.

pastry

Pastry is a mixture of flour, fat, and water. It is rolled flat and baked. Tarts and pies are made with **pastry**.

pat pats, patting, patted

When you **pat** something, you touch it gently with the palm of your hand.
*Carlos **patted** the dog on the head.*

path paths

A **path** is like a small lane for people to walk along.
*We took the **path** through the forest.*

patient patients

1 A **patient** is a sick person who is being looked after.
2 A **patient** person stays calm when things go wrong.
*Please be **patient** – dinner's a bit late today.*

pattern patterns

1 A **pattern** is a set of repeated designs.

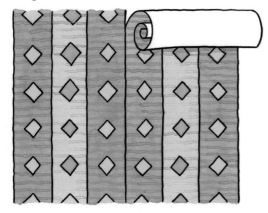

2 A **pattern** is also the way that numbers or letters are related to one another.
*Find the **pattern** in these numbers: 2, 4, 6, 8.*

paw paws

A **paw** is the foot of an animal such as a cat or a bear.

pay pays, paying, paid

If you **pay** for something, you give money for it.

PC PCs

A **PC** is a small computer that people use in offices and homes. **PC** is short for personal computer.

pea peas

A **pea** is a small, round, green vegetable. **Peas** grow in long green shells called pods.

peace

Peace is a quiet time, when no one is fighting.

peach peaches

A **peach** is a round, soft, juicy fruit. It has a large stone and a furry skin.

peacock peacocks

A **peacock** is a large blue and green male bird. It can open its tail like a fan. The female is called a peahen.

peanut peanuts

A **peanut** is a small nut. It grows in a shell under the ground.

pear pears

A **pear** is a juicy fruit that grows on a tree.

pebble pebbles

A **pebble** is a small, round stone.

peck pecks, pecking, pecked

When a bird **pecks**, it bites at something quickly with its beak.

pedal pedals, pedaling, pedaled

1 A **pedal** is part of a bike.
(See page 175.)
2 When you **pedal** a bike, you push the **pedals** with your feet.

peel peels, peeling, peeled

1 **Peel** is the skin of some fruit and vegetables.
2 When you **peel** something, you take off its skin.

a
b
c
d
e
f
g
h
i
j
k
l
m
n
o
Pp
q
r
s
t
u
v
w
x
y
z

a
b
c
d
e
f
g
h
i
j
k
l
m
n
o

Pp

q
r
s
t
u
v
w
x
y
z

pen pens
You use a **pen** when you write or draw with ink.
I drew this picture with a pen.

pencil pencils
A **pencil** is a thin stick of wood with a gray or colored center. You use a **pencil** to write or draw.

penguin penguins
A **penguin** is a black and white bird that lives where it is very cold. It cannot fly but uses its wings for swimming.

penny pennies
A **penny** is another name for cent. It is a small coin used in the United States. There are 100 **pennies** in a dollar.

pentagon pentagons
A **pentagon** is a flat shape that has five sides. (See page 184.)

people
People means more than one person. See **person**.

pepper peppers
1 **Pepper** is a powder with a hot taste used to flavor food.
2 A **pepper** is a hollow red, green or yellow vegetable. It sometimes tastes hot and spicy.

perform performs, performing, performed
1 When you **perform**, you do something in front of an audience.
The magician performed his magic tricks on the stage.
2 When you **perform** an action, you do it.

period periods
1 A **period** of time has a beginning and an end.
The rain fell for short periods of time.
2 A **period** is the dot you write at the end of a sentence.

person people
A **person** is a man, woman, or child. A **person** can also be called a human.

pest pests
A **pest** is an insect or small animal that damages plants and crops.

pet pets
A **pet** is an animal that you look after. **Pets** often live in your home.
We keep a dog, a cat, and a pony as pets.

petal petals
A **petal** is a colored part of a flower.

phone phones
You use a **phone** to speak to someone in another place. **Phone** is short for telephone.

photograph **photographs, photographing, photographed**
1 A **photograph**, or **photo**, is a picture made using a camera and film.
2 If you **photograph** something, you take a **photo** of it.

piano **pianos**
A **piano** is a large musical instrument. You press black and white keys to make music.

pick **picks, picking, picked**
1 When you **pick** something, you choose it.
2 If you **pick** a flower, you take it off its plant.
3 When you **pick** something up, you lift it.

picnic **picnics**
If you have a **picnic**, you carry a meal somewhere and eat it outside.
*We took a **picnic** to the beach.*

pictogram **pictograms**
A **pictogram** is a kind of graph. It uses pictures instead of lines.

 = 1 child

How we travel to school

Car
Bus
Walk

picture **pictures**
A **picture** is a drawing, painting, or photograph.

pie **pies**
A **pie** is fruit, meat, or other food covered in pastry and baked in the oven.

piece **pieces**
A **piece** of something is a part of it.
*Mom gave me a **piece** of apple pie.*

pier **piers**
A **pier** is a long platform built out into the sea.

pig **pigs**
A **pig** is a farm animal. It has a snout and a curly tail. The meat from a **pig** is called pork.

pigeon **pigeons**
A **pigeon** is a bird that is often seen in towns and cities.

pile **piles**
A **pile** is a number of things put on top of one another.
*Please put your clothes in a neat **pile**.*

pill **pills**
A **pill** is a kind of medicine. It is small and round so that it can be swallowed without chewing.

a
b
c
d
e
f
g
h
i
j
k
l
m
n
o
Pp
q
r
s
t
u
v
w
x
y
z

a
b
c
d
e
f
g
h
i
j
k
l
m
n
o

Pp

q
r
s
t
u
v
w
x
y
z

pillow pillows
A **pillow** is a bag filled with soft material. You rest your head on a **pillow** when you are in bed.

pilot pilots
A **pilot** flies an airplane.

pin pins
A **pin** is a short, thin piece of metal with a sharp point. You use **pins** to hold pieces of cloth together.

pineapple pineapples
A **pineapple** is a large fruit with sweet, juicy yellow flesh. It has a thick, lumpy brown skin and grows in hot countries.

pint pints
Liquids like milk can be measured in **pints**.

pipe pipes
A **pipe** is a long tube. **Pipes** carry liquids or gas from one place to another.

pirate pirates
A **pirate** is a sailor who attacks and robs other ships.

pizza pizzas
A **pizza** is a round, flat piece of bread covered with cheese, tomatoes, and other foods. It is baked in a very hot oven.

place places
1 A **place** is a piece of land or a building.
2 A **place** is where something or someone is.
*Don't move – stay in your **places**!*
3 The number 542 has a 5 in the hundreds **place**, a 4 in the tens **place**, and a 2 in the units **place**.

plain plainer, plainest
Plain means simple or without decoration.
*Emma wore a **plain** green top.*

plan plans, planning, planned
1 If you **plan** something, you decide how to do it.
2 A **plan** is a drawing or diagram of something that is to be made.

plane planes
A **plane** is a large flying vehicle that carries people or things. It has wings and one or more engines. **Plane** is short for airplane.

planet planets
A **planet** is a large, round object in space that moves around a star. Earth is a **planet** that travels around the sun once a year. Some **planets** have rings.

plant **plants, planting, planted**
1 A **plant** is anything that lives that is not an animal. Trees and flowers are **plants**. Mushrooms and grass are **plants**, too.
2 If you **plant** something, you put seeds or **plants** into the ground to grow.
*We've **planted** some poppy seeds in the garden.*

plaster **plasters**
A **plaster** is a soft, white mixture that goes hard when it dries. **Plaster** is spread on walls to make them smooth.

plastic **plastics**
Plastic is a strong, light material made in factories. It is used for buckets, bottles, plates, toys, and many other things.

plate **plates**
A **plate** is a flat dish that you put food on.

platform **platforms**
1 You stand on a **platform** so that you can be seen easily. It is higher than the rest of the room.
2 You stand on a **platform** at a railroad station to wait for a train.

play **plays, playing, played**
1 When you **play** a game, you do something for fun.
2 If you **play** a musical instrument, you make music with it.
3 A **play** is a story that is performed by actors.

playground **playgrounds**
A **playground** is a place outside where children play.

playtime
Playtime is when you come out of your house to play.

please **pleases, pleasing, pleased**
1 If you **please** someone, you make him or her happy.
2 You say **please** when you ask for something.
Please may I have an ice cream cone?

plenty
If there is **plenty** of something, there is a lot of it.
*Help yourself – there's **plenty** of food!*

plow **plows**
A **plow** is a farm tool. It cuts up the earth so that seeds can be planted.

plum **plums**
A **plum** is a small, juicy red or yellow fruit. It has a smooth skin and a stone in the middle.

plump **plumper, plumpest**
If someone or something is **plump**, they are a bit fat.
*Our cat is **plump** and cuddly.*

plural **plurals**
Plural means more than one. Many **plural** words end in the letter s.
*"Dogs" is the **plural** of "dog."*
*"Children" is the **plural** of "child."*

a
b
c
d
e
f
g
h
i
j
k
l
m
n
o

Pp

q
r
s
t
u
v
w
x
y
z

plus

Plus is another word you can use when you add. The symbol + means **plus**.

pocket   pockets

A **pocket** is a small bag sewn into clothes. You keep things in your **pockets**.

poem   poems

A **poem** is a piece of writing that uses language in a special way. It uses rhythm and often rhyme.

poet   poets

A **poet** is a person who writes poems.

poetry

Poetry means poems or a collection of poems.

point   points, pointing, pointed

1 If you **point** at something, you hold your finger toward it to show where it is.
2 The **point** of something is the sharp part at the end.

pointed

Something **pointed** has a sharp point at the end.

poisonous

If something is **poisonous**, it makes you ill if you eat or drink it.
*Some mushrooms are **poisonous**.*

polar bear   polar bears

A **polar bear** is a large white bear. It lives near the North Pole.

pole   poles

1 A **pole** is a long, thin piece of wood or metal.
*The tent was held up by metal **poles**.*
2 The North **Pole** and the South **Pole** are places at opposite ends of the Earth.
*The **Poles** are covered in ice and are the coldest places on Earth.*

police

The **police** are men and women who make sure that no one breaks the law. They are often called **policemen**, **policewomen**, or **police officers**.
*The **police** are looking for the burglars.*

polish   polishes, polishing, polished

If you **polish** something, you rub it to make it shine. You often use a cloth with **polish** on it.

polite

A **polite** person behaves well and is not rude.
*It is **polite** to hold the door open for other people.*

pond   ponds

A **pond** is a small area of water in a garden or field.

pony ponies
A **pony** is a small horse.

pool pools
1 A **pool** is a small area of still water next to the sea.
*Paul and Martha found lots of little crabs in the rock **pool**.*
2 **Pool** is also short for swimming **pool**.

poor poorer, poorest
A **poor** person does not have very much money.

pop pops, popping, popped
1 If you **pop** a balloon, it bursts with a short, sharp sound.
2 **Pop** is modern popular music.

popcorn
You eat **popcorn** as a snack with salt or butter. Seeds of corn are heated until they burst.

poppy poppies
A **poppy** is a wild plant. It has a large red flower.

popular
If something is **popular**, lots of people like it.

porridge
Porridge is a hot breakfast cereal. It is made from oats and water or milk.

position positions
1 Your **position** is where you are or how your body is arranged.
2 Your **position** is also where you play in a team.
*"What **position** do you play?" "I'm the goalkeeper."*

possible
If something is **possible**, it can be done or can happen.
*It's still **possible** to get tickets for the game.*

post posts
A **post** is a piece of wood or metal fixed upright in the ground.

poster posters
A **poster** is a large notice or picture. It is put up to tell people about something.
*Did you see the **poster** on the wall about the rock concert?*

post office post offices
A **post office** is a place where you can send letters and packages. It also sells stamps.

pot pots
A **pot** is a round container. **Pots** hold many different things, and some are used for cooking food.

a
b
c
d
e
f
g
h
i
j
k
l
m
n
o
Pp
q
r
s
t
u
v
w
x
y
z

a
b
c
d
e
f
g
h
i
j
k
l
m
n
o

q
r
s
t
u
v
w
x
y
z

potato potatoes
A **potato** is a common vegetable. It grows under the ground. Chips and French fries are made from **potatoes**.

pound pounds
You can measure weight in **pounds**. A **pound** (lb) is 12 ounces.
*My dad weighs 200 **pounds**!*

pour pours, pouring, poured
1 If you **pour** a liquid, you tip it out of its container.
2 When it is **pouring** rain, it is raining heavily.

powder
Powder is a solid material that is in very tiny pieces. Flour is a **powder**.

power
The **power** of something is its strength.
*A truck's engine has more **power** than a car's engine.*

practice practices, practicing, practiced
1 **Practice** means doing something many times to get better at it.
*Try to get lots of spelling **practice** before the test.*
2 If you **practice** something, you do it many times to get better at it.
*I am **practicing** my song for the show.*

pray prays, praying, prayed
If you **pray**, you talk to God.

predict predicts, predicting, predicted
If you **predict** something, you say it will happen in the future.

present presents
1 You give people **presents** on their birthday or at Christmas.
2 The **present** is now.
3 If you are **present** somewhere, you are there.

press presses, pressing, pressed
When you **press** something, you push hard on it.
*Mike **pressed** the doorbell.*

pretend pretends, pretending, pretended
If you **pretend**, you try to be something you are not.
*Let's **pretend** to be pirates. This tree can be our ship.*

pretty prettier, prettiest
Pretty means nice to look at.
*Those kittens are really **pretty**!*

price prices
The **price** of something is the money you pay for it.

prick pricks, pricking, pricked
If you **prick** something, you make a tiny hole using a sharp point.

prince princes
A **prince** is the son of a king or queen.

princess   princesses

1 The daughter of a king or queen is called a **princess**.
2 The wife of a prince is sometimes called a **princess**.

principal   principals

The **principal** is the person in charge of a school.

print   prints, printing, printed

When words and pictures are **printed**, they are put on the paper using a machine. Usually lots of copies are **printed** at once.
*The pages of this dictionary are **printed**.*

printer   printers

1 A **printer** prints books or newspapers using a machine.
2 A **printer** is also a machine that prints information from a computer.

prison   prisons

People who have broken the law sometimes go to **prison**.

prize   prizes

You win a **prize** if you are very good at something or by being lucky.

problem   problems

A **problem** is something that is hard to figure out.
*I've got a **problem** – my lace is broken.*

program   programs

1 A **program** is a set of instructions that tells a computer what to do.
2 A **program** is a show on television or radio.
3 A **program** is a small book of information about a show or a sports match.

project   projects

If you are doing a **project**, you find lots of information about something and then write about it.
*I did a **project** on dinosaurs at school.*

promise   promises, promising, promised

If you **promise** to do something, you mean that you really will do it.
*Mom **promised** that we'd go to the playground today.*

pronoun   pronouns

A **pronoun** is a word like "me" or "your." It is used instead of a noun. (See page 179.)

proper

Proper means right or correct.
*Put those books back in their **proper** place, please.*

a
b
c
d
e
f
g
h
i
j
k
l
m
n
o
Pp
q
r
s
t
u
v
w
x
y
z

a
b
c
d
e
f
g
h
i
j
k
l
m
n
o

Pp

q
r
s
t
u
v
w
x
y
z

protect protects, protecting, protected

If you **protect** someone or something, you keep him or it safe.

*Ruby wore a helmet to **protect** her head when she rode her bike.*

proud prouder, proudest

When you are **proud** of someone, you feel very pleased with him or her because he or she has done well.

*This school is very **proud** of the winning volleyball team.*

prove proves, proving, proved

When you **prove** something, you show that it is true.

*I can **prove** Neil wasn't there because he was at my house!*

publisher publishers

A **publisher** prints and sells books, newspapers, or magazines.

pudding puddings

A **pudding** is a sweet food that you eat at the end of a meal.

puddle puddles

A **puddle** is a small pool of water that is left after rain.

pull pulls, pulling, pulled

When you **pull** something, you hold it and make it come toward you.

pumpkin pumpkins

A **pumpkin** is a large, round, orange vegetable. People make **pumpkin** lanterns at Halloween.

punctuation

Punctuation means signs like periods, commas, and question marks. Here are some **punctuation** marks:
. , " " ' ! ?

puncture punctures

A **puncture** is a small hole made by something sharp. If a tire has a **puncture**, the air gets out and it goes flat.

*Dad fixed the **puncture** in my tire.*

punish punishes, punishing, punished

If someone is **punished**, they are made unhappy because they have done something wrong.

*Mom **punished** Jenny for being rude by sending her to her room.*

punishment punishments

A **punishment** is something unpleasant that happens to someone who has done wrong.

pupil pupils

I The **pupils** at school are the children who go there to learn.

2 The **pupil** of your eye is the black part in the middle.

puppet puppets

A **puppet** is a small toy figure of a person or animal. You move a **puppet** by pulling strings or by putting your hand inside its body.

puppy puppies

A **puppy** is a young dog.

pure purer, purest

Something that is **pure** has nothing else mixed with it.

purse purses

You keep money in a **purse**.

push pushes, pushing, pushed

If you **push** something, you move it away from you with your hands.

put puts, putting, put

When you **put** something somewhere, you place it there.

*I **put** my book in my bag.*

puzzle puzzles

A **puzzle** is something that is hard to understand or work out. People do **puzzles** for fun.

*I enjoyed doing the crossword **puzzle**.*

pyramid pyramids

I A **pyramid** is a solid shape. Its sides are triangles that meet in a point at the top.

2 The **pyramids** are huge stone buildings in Egypt.

a
b
c
d
e
f
g
h
i
j
k
l
m
n
o
Pp
q
r
s
t
u
v
w
x
y
z

quack   quacks
A **quack** is the cry of a duck. It is a loud, hard sound.

quarrel   quarrels, quarreling, quarreled
1 A **quarrel** is an angry argument.
2 When you **quarrel** with someone, you talk angrily to each other.
*My sister and I **quarreled** about who should clean out the rabbit hutch.*

quarter   quarters
1 When you divide something exactly into four, each piece is a **quarter**.

$\frac{1}{4}$

2 Quarter past ten means 15 minutes after ten o'clock. **Quarter** to ten means 15 minutes before ten o'clock.

queen   queens
1 A **queen** is a woman who rules a country because she belongs to a royal family.
2 The wife of a king is called a **queen**.

question   questions
When you ask a **question**, you want to know something.
*Who can answer Alice's **question** about the homework?*

question mark   question marks
A **question mark** is used at the end of a sentence that asks a question.
*Does this sentence need a **question mark**? Is it asking a question?*

quick   quicker, quickest
Something **quick** does not take long.
*Can I have a **quick** look at your book?*

quickly
If you do something **quickly**, you do it in very little time.

quiet   quieter, quietest
When someone is **quiet**, he or she makes very little noise.

quite
1 Quite means more than a bit.
*I am **quite** hungry but not starving.*
2 Not **quite** means nearly.
*I have not **quite** finished my writing.*

quiz   quizzes
A **quiz** is a kind of short test. People are asked questions to find out what they know.

quotation marks
Quotatiom marks are marks you use in writing to show when someone starts and stops speaking.

Rr

rabbit rabbits
A **rabbit** is a small furry animal with long ears. Wild **rabbits** live in tunnels under the ground.

race races
A **race** is a competition to see who is the fastest.
My friend won the sack race.

radiator radiators
A **radiator** is a metal container filled with liquid. It is used to heat a room.

radio radios
A **radio** turns waves in the air into programs that you can hear.
I listen to music on my radio.

raft rafts
A **raft** is a flat boat. It is made from long pieces of wood joined together.

rag rags
A **rag** is a piece of old cloth. **Rags** are used to clean or wipe things.

railway railways
A **railway** is the metal bars over which trains run.

rain rains, raining, rained
When it **rains**, little drops of water called **rain** fall from the sky.

rainbow rainbows
A **rainbow** is a band of different colors in the sky. You sometimes see a **rainbow** when the sun shines through rain. The colors of the **rainbow** are red, orange, yellow, green, blue, indigo, and violet.

raise raises, raising, raised
1 If you **raise** something, you lift it up higher.
2 If you **raise** your voice, you speak louder.

rake rakes
A **rake** is a garden tool used for collecting leaves and grass into piles. It has a row of metal or wooden teeth and a long handle.

Ramadan
Ramadan is a time when Muslims do not eat or drink during daylight hours.

ran See **run**.

a
b
c
d
e
f
g
h
i
j
k
l
m
n
o
p
q

s
t
u
v
w
x
y
z

rang See **ring**.

rare **rarer, rarest**
Something that is **rare** is not seen very often.
*This is a **rare** bird – there are only fifty in the whole world.*

raspberry **raspberries**
A **raspberry** is a small, soft, red fruit.

rat **rats**
A **rat** is an animal that looks like a large mouse. It has sharp teeth and a long tail.

rather
I If you would **rather** do something, you would like to do it more than something else.
*I'd **rather** stay in than go out.*
2 If something is **rather** cold, it is a bit cold.

rattle **rattles, rattling, rattled**
I When something **rattles**, it makes short, quick knocking sounds.
2 A **rattle** is a toy that a baby shakes to make a noise.

raw
Raw food is not cooked.
Raw carrots are sweet and crisp.

reach **reaches, reaching, reached**
I When you **reach** a place, you arrive there.
2 When you **reach** for something, you stretch out your hand toward it.
*I **reached** for a book on the top shelf.*

read **reads, reading, read**
I When you can turn written letters into words and sentences, you can **read**.
2 When you **read** aloud, you say the words that are written.
*I am **reading** a bedtime story.*

ready
If you are **ready**, you can start right away.
*I've packed my bag and I'm **ready** to go.*

real
I If something is **real**, it is a fact or it is true.
*This is a story about a **real** person who is still alive today.*
2 A **real** thing is exactly what it is meant to be and not a copy.
*This is a **real** diamond, not a piece of glass.*

really
You use **really** to show that something is true.
*Did you **really** see a monkey at the zoo?*
*I'm **really** tired.*

rearrange rearranges, rearranging, rearranged
If you **rearrange** things, you put them in a different order.

reason reasons
A **reason** tells you why something has happened.
The reason I'm late is that the bus broke down.

receive receives, receiving, received
If you **receive** something, it is sent or given to you.
I received a letter from my grandma.

recipe recipes
A **recipe** is a set of instructions. It tells you how to make something to eat or drink.

recite recites, reciting, recited
If you **recite** a poem, you say it out loud.

record records, recording, recorded
1 Someone who does something better than anybody else sets a **record**.
2 If you **record** something, you put it on tape or write it down.

recorder recorders
A **recorder** is a musical instrument. It is played by blowing into one end.

recount recounts, recounting, recounted
If you **recount** a story, you tell it.

rectangle rectangles
A **rectangle** is a shape with four sides and four corners that are all right angles. Its opposite sides are the same length.

rectangular
Anything in the shape of a rectangle is **rectangular**. A notebook is **rectangular**.

reflection reflections
1 When you look in a mirror, you see a **reflection** of yourself.

2 A **reflection** of something is also a copy where everything is the other way around.

a
b
c
d
e
f
g
h
i
j
k
l
m
n
o
p
q
Rr
s
t
u
v
w
x
y
z

refrigerator **refrigerators**
You keep food cold and fresh in a large metal container called a **refrigerator**. A **refrigerator** is often called a fridge.

refuse **refuses, refusing, refused**
If you **refuse** to do something, you say that you will not do it.
Mom asked if I would like to go shopping, but I refused.

remember **remembers, remembering, remembered**
If you **remember** something, you can bring it back to your mind.
I can remember my first day at school.

remind **reminds, reminding, reminded**
If you **remind** someone to do something, you make him or her remember to do it.
Liam reminded me to take my book home.

remove **removes, removing, removed**
If you **remove** something, you take it away.
Please remove your bags from the floor.

repair **repairs, repairing, repaired**
If you **repair** something that is broken, you fix it.

repeat **repeats, repeating, repeated**
When something is **repeated**, it happens all over again.
I'm going to watch that program again when it is repeated next week.

reply **replies, replying, replied**
1 If you **reply** to something, you give an answer.
I haven't replied to Annie's invitation yet.
2 A **reply** is the answer you give.
I haven't sent a reply yet.

report **reports**
A **report** tells you the facts about something.
We read a book on goldfish and then wrote a report on how to look after them.

represent **represents, representing, represented**
A letter or symbol that takes the place of a number or word **represents** it.

reptile **reptiles**
A **reptile** is an animal with cold blood and scaly skin. **Reptiles** have short legs or no legs at all. They usually lay eggs.

rescue **rescues, rescuing, rescued**
If you **rescue** someone, you save them from danger.
The farmer rescued the cow from the river.

rest rests, resting, rested

1 When you **rest**, you are quiet and do nothing for a while.

Jane is resting in her chair.

2 You have a **rest** when you sit or lie down quietly.

Mary always has a rest after lunch.

3 The **rest** of something is all that remains of it.

I ate half the cake and couldn't finish the rest.

restaurant restaurants

You can buy and eat a meal at a **restaurant**.

result results

A **result** is what happens because something else has happened.

Alex missed his bus, and as a result was late for school.

retell retells, retelling, retold

If you **retell** a story, you tell it again in a new way.

This story has been retold all over the world.

return returns, returning, returned

1 If you **return**, you go back to the place where you were before.

Mom has just returned home from work.

2 If you **return** something to someone, you give it back to them.

I'll return Jim's book when I've read it.

reward rewards, rewarding, rewarded

You can be given a **reward** for doing something well.

The police gave Jason a reward for finding the gold watch.

rhinoceros rhinoceroses

A **rhinoceros**, or **rhino,** is a large wild animal. It has one or two horns on its nose. **Rhinoceroses** live in Africa and Asia.

rhyme rhymes, rhyming, rhymed

1 Words that **rhyme** end with the same sound, like *bean* and *green*.

2 A **rhyme** is a short rhyming poem.

rhythm rhythms

A **rhythm** is a repeated pattern of sound in music or poetry.

ribbon ribbons

A **ribbon** is a long, narrow piece of colored material.

I put yellow ribbon around the gift.

rice

Rice is a plant that grows in hot countries. You can cook and eat the seeds of the **rice** plant.

rich richer, richest

A **rich** person has a lot of money.

riddle riddles

A **riddle** is a difficult question with a funny answer.

Here is a riddle. What gets bigger the more you take away? A hole!

ride rides, riding, rode, ridden

1 If you **ride** a bike or a horse, you sit on it and control how it moves.
2 When you **ride** in a bus, car, or train, you travel in it.

right

1 Right means the opposite of left.
*Tom has his **right** foot on the ball.*
2 Right also means correct.
*Well done! You got all your sums **right**.*
3 Right can also mean exactly.
*Stand **right** in the middle of the circle.*

right angle right angles

A **right angle** is an angle of 90 degrees. The symbol for it is a small square.
*The sides of a square meet at **right angles**.*

ring rings, ringing, rang, rung

1 A **ring** is a small circle of metal that you wear on your finger.
2 When you shake or press a bell and it makes a noise, it **rings**.

ripe riper, ripest

When fruit is **ripe**, it is ready to eat.
*That tomato is still green because it isn't **ripe** yet.*

rise rises, rising, rose, risen

1 If something **rises**, it moves upward.
2 If you **rise**, you stand up.

river rivers

A **river** is water that flows through the land to a sea or a lake.

road roads

A **road** is a long piece of hard ground. Cars and other vehicles travel along **roads**.

roar roars

A **roar** is a deep, loud noise like a lion makes.

robin robins

A **robin** is a small brown bird with a red breast.

robot robots

A **robot** is a machine controlled by a computer. **Robots** can move and do jobs that people usually do.
*A lot of cars are made by **robots**.*

rock rocks, rocking, rocked

1 Rock is the very hard material that the surface of the Earth is made of. Pieces of this are called **rocks**.
2 If you **rock** something, you move it gently from side to side.

rocket rockets

1 A **rocket** is a vehicle shaped like a pointed tube that goes into space.
2 A **rocket** is also a firework that explodes high up in the sky.

rod rods
A **rod** is a long, thin piece of wood or metal. **Rods** are used for fishing.

rode See **ride**.

roll rolls, rolling, rolled
1 When an object such as a wheel moves across a surface, it **rolls**.
2 A **roll** of something is a long piece wrapped around and around on itself. Toilet paper comes on a **roll**.
3 A bread **roll** is a small, round piece of bread.

roof roofs
The **roof** of a building or car is the top part of it.

room rooms
A **room** is part of a building. It has its own walls, floor, and ceiling.

root roots
A **root** is the part of a plant that grows under the ground.

rope ropes
Rope is a very thick, strong type of string. It is made by twisting together many threads.

rose roses
A **rose** is a beautiful garden flower with a lovely smell.

rough rougher, roughest
1 If something is **rough**, it is bumpy and not smooth.
2 **Rough** weather is stormy and not quiet.

roughly
Roughly means about but not exactly.
*I'll be there at **roughly** five o'clock.*

round
Something **round** has a shape like a circle or a ball.

route routes
Your **route** is how you get from one place to another.
*There are two **routes** from here to my house.*

row rows, rowing, rowed
1 (*sounds like* toe) A **row** is a line of things or people side by side.
2 (*sounds like* toe) When you **row** a boat, you move it through the water using oars.

3 (*sounds like* cow) When people are angry and shout at each other, they are having a **row**.

royal
Queens, kings, and members of their family are **royal**. They are all members of the **royal** family.

a
b
c
d
e
f
g
h
i
j
k
l
m
n
o
p
q

Rr

s
t
u
v
w
x
y
z

rub rubs, rubbing, rubbed
If you **rub** something, you move your hand, or something you are holding, backward and forward across it.
I rubbed my shoes until they shone.

rubber rubbers
Rubber is a strong, stretchy material. Car tires and rain boots are made of **rubber**.

ruby rubies
A **ruby** is a red jewel.

rude ruder, rudest
A **rude** person behaves badly and is not polite.
It is rude to call people names!

rug rugs
A **rug** is a small, thick carpet.

ruin ruins, ruining, ruined
I If you **ruin** something, you spoil it completely.
The rain ruined our vacation.
2 A **ruin** is a building that is almost completely destroyed.

rule rules, ruling, ruled
I A **rule** describes what you must do or what always happens.
Eating in the library is against the rules.
2 Someone who **rules** a country tells everybody else what to do.

ruler rulers
I A **ruler** is used for measuring or for drawing straight lines.

2 A **ruler** is also someone who rules a country.

run runs, running, ran, run
I When you **run**, you move quickly and both your feet come off the ground at once.
2 If you **run** a bath, you turn on the taps and fill it up.
3 A **run** is a score made in baseball.

rung See **ring**.

rush rushes, rushing, rushed
I If you **rush**, you do something or go somewhere very quickly.
We rushed to the shops before they closed.
2 If you are in a **rush**, you are busy and do not have enough time to do things.

sack sacks
A **sack** is a large bag. It is made of cloth or plastic and used to carry or store things in.
The sack of potatoes was heavy.

sad sadder, saddest
If you are **sad**, you do not feel happy.
I was very sad when we left our old house.

saddle saddles
You sit on a **saddle** when you ride a horse or a bicycle.

safe safer, safest; safes
1 If someone or something is **safe**, they are not in danger.
Lock your bike in the garage. It will be safe there.
2 A **safe** is a strong metal box with special locks. You can keep money and valuable things in a **safe**.

said See say.

sail sails, sailing, sailed
1 A **sail** is a large piece of cloth fixed onto a boat. The boat is moved through the water by the wind blowing into the **sails**.
2 If you **sail**, you travel in a boat.
We are sailing on the four o'clock ferry.

sailor sailors
A **sailor** works on a ship.

salad salads
Salad is a mixture of raw vegetables and other things, eaten cold.

sale sales
During a **sale**, shops sell things at lower prices.
Mom bought my coat for half price in the sale.

salt
Salt is a white powder that is used to flavor food. **Salt** is found in the ground and in sea water.

same
1 If two things are the **same**, they are exactly like each other.
2 If things happen at the **same** time, they happen together exactly.

sand
Sand is a powder made from very tiny bits of rock. **Sand** is found on beaches and in deserts.

sandal sandals
A **sandal** is a light, open shoe that you wear in warm weather.

a
b
c
d
e
f
g
h
i
j
k
l
m
n
o
p
q
r
Ss
t
u
v
w
x
y
z

127

a
b
c
d
e
f
g
h
i
j
k
l
m
n
o
p
q
r
Ss
t
u
v
w
x
y
z

sandbox **sandboxes**
A **sandbox** is a box filled with sand for children to dig in.

sandwich **sandwiches**
You make a **sandwich** by putting a filling between two pieces of bread.

sang See **sing**.

sank See **sink**.

sari **saris**
A **sari** is a piece of of clothing worn by Indian women. It is a long piece of material folded around the body in a special way.

sat See **sit**.

satellite **satellites**
A **satellite** is something that is sent into space to travel around the Earth. **Satellites** send back new information or pass signals from one part of the Earth to another.
The television pictures came from Australia by satellite.

Saturday **Saturdays**
Saturday is the day of the week between Friday and Sunday.

sauce **sauces**
A **sauce** is a thick, cooked liquid. It is served with food to give it more flavor.
My favorite meal is fish sticks, French fries, and peas covered in tomato sauce.

saucepan **saucepans**
A **saucepan** is is a deep metal pot with a long handle and a lid. You cook food in a **saucepan**.

saucer **saucers**
A **saucer** is a small round plate that you put a cup on.

sausage **sausages**
A **sausage** is made from very tiny pieces of meat put into a skin.

save **saves, saving, saved**
1 If you **save** someone, you stop him or her from being hurt or killed.
My mom saved me from drowning.
2 If you **save** your money, you keep it so that you can spend it later.

saw **saws**
1 A **saw** is a tool for cutting wood. It has a blade with sharp teeth.
2 *I saw a puppy at the park.* See **see**.

say **says, saying, said**
When you **say** something, you make words with your voice.

scale **scales**
1 You weigh something using a set of **scales.**
2 A fish is covered in **scales**. A **scale** is a piece of hard skin.

scare **scares, scaring, scared**
If something **scares** you, you feel frightened.

scared
When you are **scared,** you are afraid.
Our dog is scared of fireworks.

scarf **scarfs or scarves**
A **scarf** is a long piece of material. You wear it around your neck to keep you warm.

scent **scents**
The **scent** of something is what it smells like.

school **schools**
Children go to **school** to learn.

science **sciences**
When you learn about **science**, you find out about plants and animals. You also learn about materials like water and metal, and things like sound, light, and electricity.

scissors
You use **scissors** to cut paper or cloth. They have two sharp blades and handles with holes for your fingers.

score **scores, scoring, scored**
1 You **score** a goal in soccer by putting the ball into the net.
2 The number of points the teams have in a game is called the **score**.

scratch **scratches, scratching, scratched**
1 If you **scratch** something, you make marks with something sharp.
The cat scratched the table with her claws.
2 A **scratch** is a mark or small cut.

scream **screams, screaming, screamed**
If you **scream**, you give a loud, high shout because you are frightened or excited.

screech **screeches, screeching, screeched**
When something **screeches**, it makes a loud, high noise.
The brakes screeched as the car came to a sudden stop.

screen **screens**
A **screen** is the part of a television or computer where the pictures or writing appear.

screw **screws, screwing, screwed**
1 A **screw** is a thin, pointed piece of metal. It looks like a nail but you put it in by turning it with a screwdriver.
2 If you **screw** things together, you put them together using **screws**.

sea **seas**
The **sea** is the salty water that covers most of the Earth's surface.

a
b
c
d
e
f
g
h
i
j
k
l
m
n
o
p
q
r
Ss
t
u
v
w
x
y
z

a
b
c
d
e
f
g
h
i
j
k
l
m
n
o
p
q
r

Ss

t
u
v
w
x
y
z

seal seals
A **seal** is an animal with short fur. **Seals** live in the sea and on land.

search searches, searching, searched
If you **search** for something, you look carefully for it.
I've searched everywhere for my watch but I can't find it!

seashore
The **seashore** is any place beside the sea.

season seasons
The year is divided into four parts called **seasons**. The four **seasons** are called spring, summer, autumn, and winter.

seat seats
A **seat** is somewhere that you sit.

second seconds
1 A **second** is a small amount of time. There are 60 **seconds** in a minute.
2 The **second** in a list of things comes just after the first.

secret secrets
A **secret** is something that only a few people know about.
Mom's birthday party is a secret.

see sees, seeing, saw, seen
1 When you **see** something, your eyes notice it.
2 If you go to **see** someone, you visit him or her.

seed seeds
A **seed** is a small, hard object in the fruit of a plant. When it is ripe, it can grow in the ground into a new plant.

seek seeks, seeking, sought
If you **seek** something, you look for it.
The pirate was seeking the buried treasure.

seem seems, seeming, seemed
If something **seems** to be true, it looks as if it is true.
Bronwen seems shy, but she's not.
The cat seems to be hungry.

seen See see.

seesaw seesaws
A **seesaw** is an outdoor toy. One child sits at each end of a long piece of wood. They go up and down in turn.

selfish
Selfish people care only about themselves.

sell **sells, selling, sold**
When you **sell** something, you give it to someone who pays you money for it.

semicircle **semicircles**
A **semicircle** is exactly half a circle.

send **sends, sending, sent**
When you **send** something to a place, you make it go there.
Mom sent the gift to grandma's house.

sense **senses**
People have five **senses**. They can hear, see, taste, feel, and smell.

sensible
Sensible people are good at knowing what is the best thing to do.

sent See **send**.

sentence **sentences**
A **sentence** is a group of words that tells you something. When you write a **sentence**, you begin with a capital letter and end with a period.

separate **separates, separating, separated**
1 Two things that are **separate** are not connected in any way.
2 You **separate** things when you make them come apart.

September
September is the ninth month of the year. It has 30 days.

sequence **sequences**
A **sequence** is a group of things that come in a certain order.
What is the next number in the sequence 5, 10, 15?

serve **serves, serving, served**
1 If you **serve** food or drink to people, you give it to them.
2 Someone who **serves** in a shop helps people to buy what they want.

set **sets, setting, set**
1 A **set** is a group of things that belong together.
Shall we get out the chess set?
2 When something **sets**, it gets hard or firm.
We'll turn out the Jell-O when it's set.

several
Several means more than two but not many.

sew **sews, sewing, sewed, sewn**
If you **sew**, you use a needle and thread to join two things together.
Mom is sewing a button onto my coat.

sex **sexes**
People and animals are divided into two groups, males and females. These groups are called the **sexes**.

Ss

a b c d e f g h i j k l m n o p q r **Ss** t u v w x y z

131

a
b
c
d
e
f
g
h
i
j
k
l
m
n
o
p
q
r

Ss

t
u
v
w
x
y
z

shade

If you are in the **shade**, you are in a place that the sunlight does not reach.

*It's too hot. Let's sit in the **shade** of that umbrella.*

shadow   shadows

If you stand in front of the light, you make a dark shape called a **shadow**.

shake   shakes, shaking, shook, shaken

If you **shake** something, you move it quickly from side to side.

shallow   shallower, shallowest

Something **shallow** is not very deep.

Amy sat in a shallow pool.

shampoo   shampoos

Shampoo is the soapy liquid you use for washing your hair.

shape   shapes

The **shape** of something is the pattern made by its outside edges. You use words like *square, oval,* and *cone* to describe the **shapes** of things.

*You can see lots of **shapes** on page 184.*

share   shares, sharing, shared

1 When something is divided between two or more people, it is **shared**.

2 Each person gets a **share** of something that is divided between them.

shark   sharks

A **shark** is a large, powerful fish with a lot of sharp teeth. **Sharks** live in the sea.

sharp   sharper, sharpest

1 Something **sharp** can cut or prick things easily.

*A knife has a **sharp** edge.*

*A pin has a **sharp** point.*

2 A **sharp** change is very sudden.

*There was a **sharp** bend in the road.*

shave   shaves, shaving, shaved

When people **shave**, they cut the hair from their skin to make it smooth.

shed   sheds, shedding, shed

1 A **shed** is a small building. People store garden tools in a **shed**.

2 If you **shed** something, you take it off or let it fall off.

*Trees **shed** their leaves in the autumn.*

sheep   sheep

A **sheep** is a farm animal that eats grass. **Sheep** are kept for wool and meat.

sheet sheets
1 A **sheet** is a large piece of thin cloth that you put on a bed.
2 A **sheet** of paper or glass is a piece of it.

shelf shelves
A **shelf** is a long, flat piece of wood fixed to a wall. You keep things like books on **shelves**.

shell shells
A **shell** is the hard outer part of a nut, egg, or seed. Animals like snails, crabs, and tortoises have **shells**, too.
The shells you pick up on the beach used to be the shells of little creatures.

shelter shelters, sheltering, sheltered
1 A **shelter** is a place that protects you.
I stood in the bus shelter to keep dry.
2 If you **shelter** from the rain, you stay somewhere dry.

shelves See **shelf**.

shepherd shepherds
A **shepherd** looks after sheep.

shin shins
Your **shin** is the front of your leg below the knee. (See page 174.)

shine shines, shining, shone or shined
1 When something **shines**, it gives out bright light.
2 When you **shine** an object, you rub it to make it bright.

shiny shinier, shiniest
Shiny things are bright.

ship ships
A **ship** is a large boat. **Ships** carry people and things across the sea.

shirt shirts
A **shirt** is a piece of clothing that you wear on the top part of your body. It often has a collar and buttons.

shiver shivers, shivering, shivered
When you **shiver**, your body shakes, usually because you are cold.

shoe shoes
You wear **shoes** on your feet. They are usually made of leather or plastic and have a hard bottom surface.

shoelace shoelaces
A **shoelace** is used to fasten some shoes. It goes through holes in the front of the shoe and is tied in a bow.

a
b
c
d
e
f
g
h
i
j
k
l
m
n
o
p
q
r
Ss
t
u
v
w
x
y
z

133

a
b
c
d
e
f
g
h
i
j
k
l
m
n
o
p
q
r

Ss

t
u
v
w
x
y
z

shone See **shine**.

shook See **shake**.

shoot **shoots, shooting, shot**
1 If someone **shoots**, they make something go very fast out of a gun or a bow.
2 A **shoot** is the part of a plant that you see when it first comes up through the ground.

shop **shops, shopping, shopped**
1 A **shop** is a place where things are sold.
2 When you **shop**, you go to the **shops** to buy things.

shore **shores**
The **shore** is the flat land at the edge of a sea or lake.

short **shorter, shortest**
1 A **short** person is not very tall.
2 Something **short** is not very long.
*My story is very **short**, so it will only take a few minutes to read.*

shorts
Shorts are short pants that end above the knees. (See page 177.)

shot See **shoot**.

shoulder **shoulders**
Your **shoulder** is where your arm joins your body. (See page 174.)

shout **shouts, shouting, shouted**
1 If you **shout**, you call out loudly.
2 A **shout** is a loud call or cry.

show **shows, showing, showed, shown**
1 If you **show** something to someone, you let them see it.
2 If you **show** someone how to do something, you let them watch you doing it.
3 If you see a **show**, you watch something for fun.

shower **showers**
1 If you have a **shower**, you stand under a spray of water in the bathroom and wash yourself.
2 A **shower** is rain or snow that only falls for a short time.

shown See **show**.

shrink **shrinks, shrinking, shrank, shrunk**
If something **shrinks**, it becomes smaller.

shut shuts, shutting, shut
If you **shut** something, you move part of it so that it is no longer open.
Shut the door to keep out the cold.

shy shyer, shyest
A **shy** person is nervous about meeting people.
My baby sister is so shy that she cries if someone new talks to her!

sick
Someone who is **sick** is ill.
Our teacher has been away for a week because he is sick.

side sides
1 A **side** is the left or right part of something.

2 The **sides** of an object can also be its flat faces.

3 A **side** of a flat shape is the straight line between two corners.

4 A team of players in a game can be called a **side**.

sidewalk sidewalks
A **sidewalk** is a hard path at the side of a road.
Don't walk in the road! Stay on the sidewalk.

sideways
If you move **sideways**, you go to your left or right but keep facing forward.

sigh sighs, sighing, sighed
When you **sigh**, you breathe out slowly and make a sad sound. People **sigh** when they are sad, bored or tired.

sign signs
A **sign** is a notice that gives you information using words or pictures.

signal signals
1 A **signal** is a sound or action that tells people something.
When I blow my whistle, that's the signal for the end of playtime.
2 A railway **signal** tells train drivers whether they can go or must stop.

silent
If you are **silent**, you make no noise.

silk
Silk is a smooth, shiny cloth. It is made from threads spun by a silkworm.

silly sillier, silliest
A **silly** person is not being sensible.
It was silly of you to go out in the rain without a coat!

silver
Silver is a shiny, gray metal. It is often used to make rings and earrings.

a
b
c
d
e
f
g
h
i
j
k
l
m
n
o
p
q
r
Ss
t
u
v
w
x
y
z

a
b
c
d
e
f
g
h
i
j
k
l
m
n
o
p
q
r
Ss
t
u
v
w
x
y
z

sing sings, singing, sang, sung
When you **sing**, you make musical sounds with your voice.
Harry is singing his favorite song.

single
Single means only one and not more.
We won the game by a single point.

singular
You use the **singular** form of a word when you are talking about one person or thing.
The singular of "children" is "child."

sink sinks, sinking, sank, sunk
1 If something **sinks**, it moves downward through water.
2 You can wash up in the kitchen **sink**.

sip sips, sipping, sipped
If you **sip** a drink, you take it a little at a time.

sister sisters
Your **sister** is a girl who has the same parents as you.

sit sits, sitting, sat
When you **sit**, you rest your bottom on something.

size sizes
The **size** of something is how big it is.
The popcorn comes in three sizes – small, medium, and large. Which size do you want?

Small Medium Large

skate skates
A **skate** is a special boot. An ice **skate** has a blade fixed under it and a roller **skate** has wheels.
The blade on one of my ice skates is broken.

skateboard skateboards
A **skateboard** is a board on wheels. You stand on it with both feet.

skeleton skeletons
Your **skeleton** is all your bones joined up. It holds up your body.

skill skills
If you have a **skill**, you can do something well.
Reading and writing are very useful skills.

skin

Your **skin** covers the outside of your body. Animals have many different kinds of **skin**. Some fruits and vegetables have **skin**, too.

I peeled the banana and threw away the skin.

skip skips, skipping, skipped

When you **skip**, you move forward with little jumps from one foot to the other. Sometimes you **skip** with a rope.

skirt skirts

A **skirt** is a piece of clothing worn by girls and women. It hangs down from the waist. (See page 176.)

skull skulls

Your **skull** is the bony part of your head. Your brain is inside your **skull**.

sky skies

The **sky** is the space above the Earth where you see the sun, clouds, and stars.

sled sleds

You use a **sled** to slide over snow. A large **sled** is sometimes pulled by dogs.

sleep sleeps, sleeping, slept

When you **sleep**, your eyes are closed and you do not know what is happening around you.

sleeve sleeves

A **sleeve** is the part of a jacket, shirt, or blouse that covers your arm.

slept See **sleep**.

slice slices

A **slice** is a thin piece cut from something bigger.

May I have another slice of bread, please?

slide slides, sliding, slid

1 When something **slides**, it moves quickly over a smooth surface.

2 A **slide** is an outdoor toy. You climb to the top and **slide** down.

slip slips, slipping, slipped

If you **slip**, you fall down because you slide by accident.

slipper slippers

Slippers are soft shoes that you wear indoors.

slippery

If something is **slippery**, it is difficult to hold or walk on because it is wet or very smooth.

On an icy day, the playground is very slippery.

a b c d e f g h i j k l m n o p q r **Ss** t u v w x y z

slope

a
b
c
d
e
f
g
h
i
j
k
l
m
n
o
p
q
r

Ss

t
u
v
w
x
y
z

slope slopes
A **slope** is a piece of ground or a surface that is higher at one end than the other.

slow slower, slowest
If something is **slow**, it takes a long time.

slowly
If you do something **slowly**, you take a long time to do it.

slug slugs
A **slug** is a small animal that moves slowly. It is like a snail without its shell.

small smaller, smallest
A **small** person or thing is not very big.
A mouse is a small animal.

smart smarter, smartest
1 **Smart** means clever, intelligent.
2 If you look **smart**, you look neat and well-dressed.

smash smashes, smashing, smashed
If something **smashes**, it breaks into lots of pieces.
Dad dropped the cup and it smashed on the floor.

smell smells, smelling, smelled
1 When you **smell** something, you notice it with your nose.
I could smell something burning.
2 You notice a **smell** by using your nose.
There was a smell of burning.

smile smiles, smiling, smiled
1 When you **smile**, your face looks happy.
2 A **smile** is a look of happiness on your face.

smoke
Smoke is the white or gray cloud that goes into the air when something burns.
When dad lit the bonfire, smoke filled the air.

smooth smoother, smoothest
If something is **smooth**, it has no lumps or rough bits.
Toads have bumps, but frogs are smooth.

snack snacks
A **snack** is a small, quick meal.
We had a couple of sandwiches as a snack.

snail snails
A **snail** is a small, soft creature with a shell on its back. It moves very slowly.

138

snake snakes

A **snake** is a long, thin reptile with scales and no legs. Some **snakes** are dangerous to humans.

snap snaps, snapping, snapped

If something **snaps**, it breaks suddenly with a sharp noise.
A twig snapped under my foot.

sneeze sneezes, sneezing, sneezed

When you **sneeze**, you suddenly push air out through your nose, making a loud noise.
I had a bad cold and couldn't stop sneezing.

snow snows, snowing, snowed

1 Snow is soft, white frozen water that falls from the sky when it is cold.
2 It **snows** when **snow** falls from the sky.

snowball snowballs

A **snowball** is a small ball of snow. People make **snowballs** and throw them at each other for fun.

snowflake snowflakes

A **snowflake** is a single piece of snow as it falls.

snowman snowmen

A **snowman** is snow made into the shape of a person.

soak soaks, soaking, soaked

If you **soak** something, you leave it in liquid.
Mom soaked my dirty socks in water overnight.

soap soaps

You use **soap** and water to wash yourself or your clothes.

sock socks

You wear **socks** on your feet to keep them warm. (See page 177.)

sofa sofas

A **sofa** is a long, soft seat with arms and a back. Two or three people can sit on a **sofa**.

soft softer, softest

If something is **soft**, it sinks down when you press it.
My head sank into the soft pillow.

soil

Soil is the top layer of earth that plants grow in.

Ss

a b c d e f g h i j k l m n o p q r
t u v w x y z

139

a
b
c
d
e
f
g
h
i
j
k
l
m
n
o
p
q
r
Ss
t
u
v
w
x
y
z

sold See **sell**.

soldier soldiers
A **soldier** belongs to an army.

solid
1 A **solid** material feels firm and does not change shape easily.
*Wood is **solid** but oil and water are liquid.*
2 Something **solid** is not hollow.

solve solves, solving, solved
If you **solve** a problem, you find the answer to it.

some
You say **some** when you mean a number or amount but do not say it exactly.
*Please pass me **some** sausages and **some** mashed potatoes.*

somebody
Somebody is a person you do not name.
Somebody has left his coat behind.

someone
Someone is another word for somebody.

something
Something is a thing that you do not describe.
*I can hear **something** banging.*

sometimes
Sometimes means quite often but not always.
*I'm **sometimes** allowed to stay up late when I'm on vacation.*

somewhere
If you say you went **somewhere**, you do not say exactly where.

son sons
A person's **son** is his or her male child.
*Mr. Jones has two **sons**.*

song songs
When you sing a **song**, you sing words to a piece of music.

soon sooner, soonest
Soon means not too long into the future.
*Today is Friday. **Soon** it will be the weekend.*

sore
If part of your body is **sore**, it hurts.
*I have a **sore** throat – it hurts when I swallow.*

sorry
You say that you are **sorry** when you have done something wrong.
*I'm **sorry** I'm late.*

sort sorts, sorting, sorted
1 If things are the same **sort**, they are the same kind.
*Do you like this **sort** of chocolate?*
2 If you **sort** things, you put them into groups.
Sort these buttons into two piles – red ones and blue ones.

sought See **seek**.

sound sounds
A **sound** is something you can hear.
*Can you hear the **sound** of the drums?*

soup soups
Soup is a hot liquid food made from meat or vegetables.

sour
If something is **sour**, it has a sharp taste like a lemon.
*This milk tastes **sour**. Throw it away.*

south
South is a direction. It is on your right when you look toward the rising sun.

space spaces
1 A **space** is a gap or an empty place.
*Is there a **space** for me at your table?*
2 **Space** is all around the Earth where the planets and the stars are.

spaceship spaceships
A **spaceship** is a vehicle that can travel through space.

spade spades
A **spade** is a tool used for digging. It has a long handle and a wide blade.

sparrow sparrows
A **sparrow** is a small brown bird found in many parts of the world.

speak speaks, speaking, spoke, spoken
When you **speak**, you say words out loud.

special
If something is **special**, it is better than other things of the same kind.
*Mom made a **special** meal for my birthday.*

speech
Speech is what you hear when someone is speaking.

speed speeds
The **speed** of something is how fast it is moving.
*The race car was traveling at a very high **speed**.*

spell spells, spelling, spelled or spelt
1 When you **spell** a word, you say or write the letters in the right order.
*Please **spell** your name.*
2 In fairy tales, if someone casts a **spell**, magic things happen.

spend spends, spending, spent
1 You **spend** money when you buy something with it.
2 You **spend** time when you use it.
*I **spent** three hours painting.*

a
b
c
d
e
f
g
h
i
j
k
l
m
n
o
p
q
r

Ss

t
u
v
w
x
y
z

sphere spheres

A **sphere** is an object that is round when you look at it from any direction. Soccer balls and planets are **spheres**.

spider spiders

A **spider** is a small animal with eight legs. It spins a web to catch insects for food.

spill spills, spilling, spilled

If you **spill** something, it runs out of a container by mistake.
I spilled my drink all over my shirt!

spin spins, spinning, spun

If something **spins**, it turns around very quickly.
The washing machine spins our clothes.

spine spines

1 Your **spine** is the long row of bones down the middle of your back.
2 A **spine** is a long, sharp point on an animal's body or on a plant.

spiteful

A **spiteful** person says nasty things to people.

splash splashes

When something hits the water, it makes a **splash**.

split splits, splitting, split

If something **splits**, it divides into parts.

spoil spoils, spoiling, spoiled

If something is **spoiled**, it is not as good as it was before.

spoke See **speak**.

spoon spoons

You use a **spoon** to eat soup and cereal, and to stir liquids.

sport sports

A **sport** is something that you do to keep fit and to have fun. Swimming, running, and football are all **sports**.

spot spots

1 A **spot** is a round mark.
A ladybug is red with black spots.
2 A **spot** is also a small stain on your clothes.

spout spouts

You pour the water out of a jug or kettle through its **spout**.

spray **sprays, spraying, sprayed**
If you **spray** something, you make it wet with tiny drops of liquid.

spring **springs**
1 **Spring** is the season between winter and summer. The weather gets warmer and plants start to grow again.
2 A **spring** is a curly piece of metal. It jumps back to its normal shape after you press it down.

spun See **spin**.

square **squares**
1 A **square** is a shape with four equal sides and four corners that are all right angles.
2 Anything that has this shape is **square**.

squash **squashes, squashing, squashed**
1 **Squash** is a vegetable used in soups and salads.
2 If you **squash** something, you press it so that it goes flat.
Emily sat on her hat and squashed it flat.

squeak **squeaks, squeaking, squeaked**
If something **squeaks**, it makes a short, high noise.
My new shoes squeak when I walk.

squeeze **squeezes, squeezing, squeezed**
If you **squeeze** something, you press its sides together.
Mom squeezed the oranges to get the juice out.

squirrel **squirrels**
A **squirrel** is a small animal with a long, thick tail. **Squirrels** live in trees and eat nuts.

stable **stables**
A horse is kept in a **stable**.

stage **stages**
A **stage** is a raised platform in a theater or hall.
At the play, there was a horse on the stage.

stair **stairs**
Stairs are a set of steps inside a building. You climb the **stairs** from one floor to the next.

stamp **stamps**
A **stamp** is a small piece of paper with a picture on it. You stick a **stamp** on a letter or package before you mail it.

stand **stands, standing, stood**
When you **stand**, your feet stay in one place on the floor.

a b c d e f g h i j k l m n o p q r **Ss** t u v w x y z

143

a
b
c
d
e
f
g
h
i
j
k
l
m
n
o
p
q
r

Ss

t
u
v
w
x
y
z

star stars

1 A **star** is a tiny light in the sky at night.

2 A **star** is also a famous actor or performer.

3 A **star** can also be a shape with five or more points. (See page 184.)

stare stares, staring, stared

1 If you **stare** at something, you look at it for a long time.

2 A **stare** is a long look at something.

start starts, starting, started

If you **start** to do something, you begin to do it.

*I've just **started** my homework.*

station stations

1 Trains and buses stop for passengers at a **station**.

2 A **station** is also a building with a special use, like a police **station**.

*We went to the gas **station** for some gas.*

statue statues

A **statue** is a figure of a person or animal. **Statues** are made from stone or metal.

stay stays, staying, stayed

1 If you **stay** in a place, you do not move away from it.

2 If you **stay** in a hotel, you sleep there.

steady steadier, steadiest

If something is **steady**, it does not shake or move.

*Please hold the ladder **steady**.*

steal steals, stealing, stole, stolen

If you **steal** something, you take something that belongs to someone else.

steam

Steam is the white cloud you see above very hot water. It is made of tiny drops of water.

Steam was coming off the hot tea.

steel

Steel is a strong metal.

steep steeper, steepest

A **steep** slope goes up sharply.

*We pushed our bikes up the hill because it was too **steep** to ride them.*

stem stems

The **stem** of a plant holds the leaves and flowers away from the soil.

step steps, stepping, stepped

1 You **step** when you move your foot up and down when you walk.

2 A **step** is also where you put your foot on the stairs or a ladder.

*Karen's staircase has 12 **steps**.*

stereo **stereos**

A **stereo** is a machine for playing tapes and CDs.

---

stick **sticks, sticking, stuck**

1 A **stick** is a long, thin piece of wood.

2 If you **stick** one thing to another, you fix it with glue or tape.

3 If you **stick** a pointed object into something, you push it in so that it stays there.

---

stiff **stiffer, stiffest**

If something is **stiff**, it is hard to bend.

The boxes were made of stiff cardboard.

---

still

1 If something is **still** happening, it has not stopped yet.

It's been raining all day and it's still raining.

2 If you are **still**, you are not moving.

Stand still while I button your coat.

---

sting **stings, stinging, stung**

If something **stings** you, it pricks your skin and hurts you.

A bee stung Anya in the arm.

---

stir **stirs, stirring, stirred**

When you **stir** a liquid, you use a spoon or a stick to move it around.

---

stole See **steal**.

---

stolen See **steal**.

---

stomach **stomachs**

When you swallow your food, it goes into your **stomach**.

---

stone **stones**

1 **Stone** is a hard, dry material. It is used for building houses and walls. You find small **stones** on the ground.

2 The hard seed in the middle of a peach or a plum is called a **stone**.

---

stood See **stand**.

---

stop **stops, stopping, stopped**

1 If you **stop** doing something, you do not do it any more.

2 If someone **stops** you from doing something, they do not let you do it.

3 A bus lets people on or off at a bus **stop**.

---

store **stores, storing, stored**

1 If you **store** something, you keep it until it is needed.

2 A **store** is a business that sells lots of different things.

---

storm **storms**

In a **storm** it rains hard and strong winds blow. There is often thunder and lightning.

a
b
c
d
e
f
g
h
i
j
k
l
m
n
o
p
q
r
Ss
t
u
v
w
x
y
z

145

a
b
c
d
e
f
g
h
i
j
k
l
m
n
o
p
q
r

Ss

t
u
v
w
x
y
z

story stories
A **story** tells you about people and what happened to them. Some **stories** are made up; others are about real people.

stove stoves
A **stove** is a machine for cooking food.

straight straighter, straightest
Something **straight** is not bent or curved.
*Lisa has **straight** hair.*

strange stranger, strangest
Something **strange** seems odd and unusual.
*The alien had **strange** yellow eyes.*

straw straws
1 Farm animals sleep on **straw**. It is the dry stems from wheat and corn.
2 A **straw** is a thin plastic tube that you can drink through.

strawberry strawberries
A **strawberry** is a small, soft, red fruit. It has tiny seeds on its surface.

stream streams
A **stream** is a small river.

street streets
A **street** is a road in a town. It has shops and houses along it.

street fair street fairs
A **street fair** is an outdoor show. There are things to buy, to eat, and to drink.
*We went to the **street fair** on Saturday.*

strength
Your **strength** is your energy and power.
*I haven't got the **strength** to lift that suitcase.*

stretch stretches, stretching, stretched
When you **stretch** something, you pull it to make it longer or wider.
*David **stretched** the rubber band.*

strict stricter, strictest
A **strict** person makes people behave well and do what they should.

string strings
1 **String** is thin rope used for tying things together.
2 You play on the **strings** of violins and guitars to make music.

strip strips
A **strip** is a long, thin piece of something.

stripe stripes
A **stripe** is a line on something.
*Zebras have **stripes** on their bodies.*

stroller **strollers**
A **stroller** is a small folding chair on wheels. Little children are taken around in **strollers**.

strong **stronger, strongest**
1 A **strong** person can lift heavy things.
2 You cannot easily break something that is **strong**.

stuck See **stick**.

stung See **sting**.

submarine **submarines**
A **submarine** is a ship that can travel underwater.

subtract **subtracts, subtracting, subtracted**
If you **subtract** one number from another, you take it away and count what is left. The symbol − means **subtract**, or minus.
Subtracting two from three leaves one.
$3 - 2 = 1$

subtraction
Subtraction is what you do when you take one number from another and count what is left.

succeed **succeeds, succeeding, succeeded**
If you **succeed**, you do what you have tried to do.
*Becky **succeeded** in getting onto the team.*

suck **sucks, sucking, sucked**
If you **suck** something, you pull at it with your mouth.

sudden
If something is **sudden**, it happens without warning.
*The dog gave a **sudden** bark.*

suddenly
If something happens **suddenly**, you are not expecting it to happen.
*The lights **suddenly** went out.*

sugar
Sugar is used to make food and drink sweet.

suit **suits**
A **suit** is pants or a skirt worn with a jacket of the same material.

suitcase **suitcases**
When you go on vacation, you carry your clothes in a **suitcase**.

sum **sums**

The **sum** of two or more numbers is what they make when you add them together.

13+5=18

summer

Summer is the season between spring and autumn. The weather is warm and the days are long.

sun

The **sun** is a star. It shines in the sky during the day and gives us heat and light. The Earth travels around the **sun** once a year.

Sunday **Sundays**

Sunday is the day of the week between Saturday and Monday.

sung See **sing**.

sunk See **sink**.

sunny **sunnier, sunniest**

When the weather is **sunny**, the sun is shining brightly.

sunshine

The light that comes from the sun is called **sunshine**.

supermarket **supermarkets**

A **supermarket** is a very large shop that sells food and other things. You take what you want as you go around and pay for it on the way out.

surface **surfaces**

The **surface** of something is the top or outside of it.
The surface of the table was very shiny.

surprise **surprises, surprising, surprised**

1 A **surprise** is something that you did not expect.
2 You **surprise** someone when you do something they were not expecting.
We surprised my mom by bringing her breakfast in bed.

swallow **swallows, swallowing, swallowed**

1 When you **swallow** something, it goes down your throat and into your stomach.
2 A **swallow** is also a bird. It has a forked tail.

swam See **swim**.

swan **swans**
A **swan** is a very large white bird with a long curved neck. **Swans** live on rivers or lakes.

sweater **sweaters**
A **sweater** is a piece of clothing with sleeves. You wear it on the top half of your body to keep you warm.

sweep **sweeps, sweeping, swept**
You **sweep** a floor with a broom to make it clean.

swim **swims, swimming, swam, swum**
You **swim** by using your arms and legs to move through the water.

swimming pool
swimming pools
A **swimming pool** is a large hole in the ground that is filled with water for swimming.

swing **swings, swinging, swung**
1 A **swing** is a seat hung on chains or ropes. It moves backward and forward when you push it.
2 When something **swings**, it moves backward and forward in the air.

switch **switches**
You press on a **switch** to start a machine or turn on a light.

sword **swords**
A **sword** is a long metal blade with a handle. People fought with **swords** many years ago.

syllable **syllables**
A **syllable** is a word or part of a word that has one separate sound when you say it.
*"Girl" has one **syllable** and "sister" has two **syllables**.*

synonym **synonyms**
A **synonym** is a word that means the same or almost the same as another word. (See page 180.)

syrup
Syrup is a sweet, thick liquid made by boiling sugar with water.

a b c d e f g h i j k l m n o p q r **Ss** t u v w x y z

a b c d e f g h i j k l m n o p q r s **Tt** u v w x y z

table tables
1 A **table** is a flat surface with legs. You can work or eat at a **table**.

2 A **table** is also a way of showing information.

Day	Weather
Monday	Sunny
Tuesday	Rainy and cool
Wednesday	Showers

tadpole tadpoles
A **tadpole** is a tiny black animal that lives in water. It grows into a frog.

tail tails
An animal's **tail** grows at the back end of its body.
*A dog wags its **tail** when it is happy.*

take takes, taking, took, taken
1 When you **take** something, you move it from a place.
2 If you **take** one number away from another, you subtract it and count what is left. **Take away** means the same as subtract.

tale tales
A **tale** is an old word for a story.

talk talks, talking, talked
When you **talk**, you say words out loud.

tall taller, tallest
The top of a **tall** person or object is a long way from the ground.

tally tallies
If you keep a **tally**, you record the number of times something happens.

tame tamer, tamest
A **tame** animal is friendly toward humans.
*Charlotte's **tame** lamb follows her everywhere.*

tank tanks
1 A **tank** is a large container for liquids like gasoline or water.
2 A **tank** is also a large fighting vehicle. It has a gun on top.

tap taps, tapping, tapped
1 You turn on a **tap** to run water into a sink or a bath.
2 If you **tap** something, you hit it gently.
*Mike **tapped** me on the shoulder and said hello.*

tape tapes
1 Tape is a roll of sticky ribbon. You can use it to fasten something.
2 You can record sound or pictures onto **tape**.
*We need a new **tape** for the video recorder.*

tape measure tape measures
A **tape measure** is a strip of cloth or soft plastic marked into units. It is used for measuring.

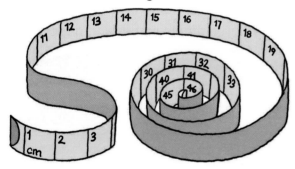

tart tarts
A **tart** is a round pastry case with a filling. It is often filled with fruit.

taste tastes, tasting, tasted
If you **taste** something, you put it in your mouth to find out what it is like to eat.

taught See **teach**.

taxi taxis
A **taxi** is a car that you pay to travel in.

tea
Tea is a hot drink. You make it by pouring boiling water onto dried leaves or a tea bag.

teach teaches, teaching, taught
If you **teach** someone, you show them how to do something.
*Can you **teach** me how to ride a bike?*

teacher teachers
A **teacher** helps people to learn something or shows them how to do something.

team teams
A **team** is a group of people who play or work together.

tear tears, tearing, tore, torn
1 (*sounds like* **hair**) If you **tear** something, you pull it apart.
2 (*sounds like* **here**) A **tear** is a drop of liquid that falls from your eye when you cry.

teaspoon teaspoons
A **teaspoon** is a small spoon used for stirring drinks.
*Add two **teaspoons** of sugar.*

teddy teddies
A **teddy**, or **teddy bear**, is a soft toy bear.

a
b
c
d
e
f
g
h
i
j
k
l
m
n
o
p
q
r
s
Tt
u
v
w
x
y
z

a
b
c
d
e
f
g
h
i
j
k
l
m
n
o
p
q
r
s

Tt

u
v
w
x
y
z

teeth See **tooth**.

telephone telephones
You use a **telephone** to speak to someone in another place.

television televisions
A **television** turns waves in the air into pictures and sounds. It is often called a TV.

tell tells, telling, told
If you **tell** someone about something, you share what you know with them.

temple temples
A **temple** is a place where some people go to pray.

tent tents
You can sleep outdoors in a **tent**. It is made from a piece of cloth stretched over metal poles.

terrible
Something **terrible** is very frightening or nasty.
*There was a **terrible** storm last night.*

test tests
When you take a **test**, you answer questions to show what you can do.

text texts
The words in a book or poem are its **text**.

The little mouse just sat quietly and waited and waited, but nobody came. The next day

just as he was waking up, he heard a footstep and a voice said, "Are you there, Sammy?"

thank thanks, thanking, thanked
You **thank** someone who has given you something or has done something for you.
Thank you for my new shirt, grandma!

theater theaters
You go to a **theater** to see a show, a play, or a movie.

theme themes
The **theme** of a story is the important thought that runs through it.

then
1 If something happened **then**, it happened at that time.
*We were living in our old house **then**.*
2 Then also tells you what happened next.
*First we watched a really good video, **then** we had dinner.*

thick thicker, thickest
1 If something is **thick**, it is a long distance from one side to the other.
*Jason likes **thick** bread but Katy prefers thin slices.*

2 A **thick** liquid flows slowly.

thief thieves
A **thief** is someone who steals things.

thigh thighs
Your **thigh** is the part of your leg between your knee and your hip.
(See page 174.)

thin thinner, thinnest
1 Something is **thin** if there is only a short distance from one side to the other.
2 A **thin** person is not fat.

thing things
A **thing** is something that is not alive.

think thinks, thinking, thought
When you **think**, you use your brain to work something out.

thirsty thirstier, thirstiest
If you are **thirsty**, you need a drink.

thought See think.

thousand thousands
A **thousand** is the number 1000. It is ten hundreds.

thread threads
A **thread** is a fine string. You use it to sew things together.

threw See throw.

throat throats
Your **throat** is the front part of your neck.

through
If you go **through** something, you go from one side of it to the other.

throw throws, throwing, threw, thrown
When you **throw** something, you use your hand to make it travel through the air.

thumb thumbs
Your **thumb** is the short finger on the inside of your hand.
(See page 174.)

thunder
Thunder is the sound that follows lightning during a storm.

thunderstorm thunderstorms
In a **thunderstorm**, there is thunder and lightning.

a b c d e f g h i j k l m n o p q r s **Tt** u v w x y z

153

a
b
c
d
e
f
g
h
i
j
k
l
m
n
o
p
q
r
s
Tt
u
v
w
x
y
z

Thursday **Thursdays**
Thursday is the day of the week between Wednesday and Friday.

tick **ticks**
1 A **tick** is a mark written ✔. It shows that an answer is correct.
2 The **tick** of a clock is the sound it makes every second.
3 A tick is also a tiny spider that may live on the skin of people or animals.
Ticks suck blood and spread disease!

ticket **tickets**
You buy a **ticket** to travel on a bus, train, or plane. You also often need a **ticket** to go to something.
*I've got two **tickets** for the concert.*

tidy **tidier, tidiest**
If a room is **tidy**, everything is neat and in the right place.

tie **ties, tying, tied**
1 You **tie** things together by making a knot or a bow.

2 People wear a **tie** around the neck of a shirt. (See page 177.)

tiger **tigers**
A **tiger** is a fierce wild cat with orange fur and black stripes. **Tigers** live in Asia.

tight **tighter, tightest**
If something is **tight**, it fits closely.
*These pants are too **tight**.*

tights
Tights cover your legs from your waist down to your feet. They are worn mainly by girls and women.

till
Till means until.
*I'll stay **till** your dad comes home.*

time
Seconds, minutes, hours, days, weeks, months, and years are all measures of **time**. (See page 178.)

timer **timers**
A **timer** is a kind of clock. It can be set to measure the time left until something happens.
*I've set the **timer** to ring after ten minutes.*

times
Times is another way of saying multiplied by. The symbol × means **times**.
*Three **times** two equals six.* $3 \times 2 = 6$

tiny **tinier, tiniest**
Something **tiny** is very small.

tip **tips**
1 A **tip** is a piece of helpful information.
2 The **tip** of something is the very end of it.
*Can you touch your nose with the **tip** of your tongue?*

tire **tires**
A **tire** is a piece of thick rubber that goes around a wheel.

tired
If you are **tired**, you need to go to sleep.

title **titles**
The **title** of a book or poem is what the writer has called it.
The title of this book is Barron's First School Dictionary.

toad **toads**
A **toad** is an animal like a large frog.

toast
Toast is a slice of bread that is cooked until it is light brown. It is often eaten with butter.

today
Today is the day you are in now.
It is my birthday today.

toe **toes**
You have five **toes** on the end of each foot. (See page 174.)

toffee **toffees**
Toffee is a chewy candy.

toilet **toilets**
You go to the **toilet** to empty waste from your body.

told See **tell**.

tomato **tomatoes**
A **tomato** is a red fruit. You often eat it raw.

tomorrow
Tomorrow is the day that comes after today.

tongue **tongues**
Your **tongue** is inside your mouth. You use it when you speak or eat.
My sister likes to stick out her tongue.

tongue twister
tongue twisters
A **tongue twister** is difficult to say quickly and correctly.
"Twin-screw steel cruiser" is a well-known tongue twister.

tonight
Tonight means the end of today.
Will you come with me to the game tonight?

took See **take**.

tool **tools**
You use a **tool** to make or fix things.
My dad uses special tools when he repairs the car.

tooth **teeth**
You have hard, white, bony **teeth** inside your mouth. You use them when you chew or bite.

toothbrush **toothbrushes**
You use a **toothbrush** to clean your teeth.

a
b
c
d
e
f
g
h
i
j
k
l
m
n
o
p
q
r
s
Tt
u
v
w
x
y
z

toothpaste

a b c d e f g h i j k l m n o p q r s

Tt

u v w x y z

toothpaste
You spread **toothpaste** on a toothbrush when you clean your teeth.

top tops
The **top** of something is its highest part.
*They climbed to the very **top** of the mountain.*

tore See **tear**.

torn See **tear**.

tortoise tortoises
A **tortoise** is a reptile with a shell on its back. It moves very slowly.

toss tosses, tossing, tossed
When you **toss** something, you throw it in the air.

total totals
When you add things up, you work out their **total**.

touch touches, touching, touched
1 When you **touch** something, you put your hand on it.
2 When things **touch**, they are placed against each other.

tough tougher, toughest
Tough means very strong and not easily broken.

tow tows, towing, towed
If you **tow** something, you pull it along behind you.
*The car **towed** a trailer.*

towel towels
You dry yourself with a **towel**.

tower towers
A **tower** is a tall building. It is often part of another building.

town towns
A **town** is a collection of homes and businesses. It is larger than a village and smaller than a city.

toy toys
A **toy** is something that you play with for fun.

trace traces, tracing, traced
When you **trace** something, you make a copy by drawing over it through a piece of clear paper.

track tracks
1 A **track** is a path for people or animals.
2 Railroad trains run on **tracks** made from long strips of metal.

tractor tractors
A **tractor** is a vehicle that is used on a farm.

traffic
Traffic is all the vehicles on the roads at one time.

traffic light traffic lights
Traffic lights tell traffic when to go or stop. They are red, yellow, and green.

trail trails
A **trail** is a path or marks that you can follow.

train trains
A **train** is an engine and cars that run on railroad tracks.

trap traps, trapping, trapped
If you are **trapped**, you are in a place that you cannot get out of.

travel travels, traveling, traveled
When you **travel**, you go on a journey.

treasure treasures
A **treasure** is something valuable.

tree trees
A **tree** is a large plant. It has a wooden trunk and branches with leaves on.

triangle triangles
A **triangle** is a flat shape with three sides.

triangular
Anything in the shape of a triangle is **triangular**.

trick tricks, tricking, tricked
1 If you **trick** someone, you make them believe something that is not true.
2 A **trick** is also a piece of magic.

tried See **try**.

tries See **try**.

trim trims, trimming, trimmed
If you **trim** something, you cut it to make it neat.
*Dad is **trimming** the hedge.*

trip trips, tripping, tripped
1 If you **trip** over something, you catch your foot on it and fall over.
2 If you go on a **trip**, you travel somewhere.
*Lou is going on a **trip** to a museum.*

trouble
1 You get into **trouble** if you do something wrong.
*If I'm home late I'll get into **trouble**.*
2 If you have **trouble**, you have a problem.

a
b
c
d
e
f
g
h
i
j
k
l
m
n
o
p
q
r
s
Tt
u
v
w
x
y
z

truck trucks
A **truck** is a large vehicle. It carries big things by road.

true truer, truest
If something is **true**, it really happened.

trumpet trumpets
A **trumpet** is a musical instrument made of metal. You blow through it to make a sound.

trunk trunks
1 The part of a tree that grows up from the ground is called a **trunk**.
2 An elephant's long nose is called a **trunk**.

3 A **trunk** is part of a car. (See page 175.)

trust trusts, trusting, trusted
If you **trust** people, you believe they will do what they say.

truth
When you tell the **truth,** you say what really happened.

try tries, trying, tried
When you **try** to do something, you do it as well as you can.

T-shirt T-shirts
A **T-shirt** is a soft cotton shirt with short sleeves and no collar.

tube tubes
A **tube** is a hollow cylinder.

tuck tucks, tucking, tucked
If you **tuck** someone in, you make them comfortable in bed.

Tuesday Tuesdays
Tuesday is the day of the week between Monday and Wednesday.

tug-of-war
A **tug-of-war** is a contest. Two teams pull on the ends of a rope. The winners pull the other side over the winning line.

tumble tumbles, tumbling, tumbled
You **tumble** when you fall head over heels.
*Jack fell down and Jill came **tumbling** after him.*

tummy **tummies**
Tummy is another word for stomach. When you swallow your food, it goes into your **tummy**.

tune **tunes**
A **tune** is the notes that go together to make a piece of music.
*That song has a **tune** that is easy to remember.*

tunnel **tunnels**
A **tunnel** is a long hole through the ground.

turn **turns, turning, turned**
1 When you **turn**, you move to your left or your right.
2 If people take **turns**, they do something one after another.
3 If something **turns** into something else, it changes.
*Water **turns** into ice when it freezes.*

turnip **turnips**
A **turnip** is a round vegetable that is white or yellow inside.

tusk **tusks**
A **tusk** is a large horn on the head of an elephant or rhinoceros.

TV **TVs**
TV is short for television.

twice
Twice means two times.
*Knock **twice** and then wait.*
__Twice__ 3 is 6.

twig **twigs**
A **twig** is a small branch of a tree or bush.

twin **twins**
When a mother has **twins**, she has two babies at the same time. **Twins** often look alike.

twist **twists, twisting, twisted**
When you **twist** something, you bend it into a round shape.

tying See **tie**.

type **types, typing, typed**
1 When you **type** something, you use a keyboard to print letters.
2 A **type** is one kind of a thing.
*What **type** of shoes do you like best?*

a
b
c
d
e
f
g
h
i
j
k
l
m
n
o
p
q
r
s
Tt
u
v
w
x
y
z

a
b
c
d
e
f
g
h
i
j
k
l
m
n
o
p
q
r
s
t
Uu
v
w
x
y
z

ugly uglier, ugliest
Something **ugly** is not nice to look at.

umbrella umbrellas
You put up an **umbrella** to keep you dry when it rains.

uncle uncles
Your **uncle** is the brother of your mother or father. Your aunt's husband is also your **uncle**.

underground
Underground means under the ground.

undershirt undershirts
An **undershirt** is a piece of clothing. It is worn under a shirt. (See page 177.)

understand understands, understanding, understood
If you **understand** something, you know what it means.

undress undresses, undressing, undressed
When you **undress**, you take your clothes off.

uniform uniforms
Some people wear a **uniform** to show what job they do or where they go to school.

unit units
The **units** of a number are the ones. *The number 37 has three tens and seven units.*

universe
The **universe** is space and all the stars and planets.

until
Until means up to a certain time.

upset
If you are **upset**, you are sad and may feel like crying.

upside down
If something is **upside down**, its top is where its bottom should be.

upstairs
If you go **upstairs**, you go up to a higher level of a building.

urgent
Something **urgent** must be done at once.

use uses, using, used
Something is **used** to do a job.

useful
Something **useful** is used to do a job.

usual
Something **usual** happens most of the time.

usually
Usually means often but not always.

Vv

vacuum cleaner
vacuum cleaners
A **vacuum cleaner**
is a machine
that sucks
up dust.

valley **valleys**
A **valley** is a low area of land
between hills or mountains.

valuable
Something **valuable** is worth a lot of
money.
The thief stole a valuable clock.

van **vans**
A **van** is a vehicle for carrying things
or people.

vanish **vanishes, vanishing,**
vanished
If something **vanishes**, you suddenly
cannot see it any more.
I had my pencil a minute ago but now it's
vanished!

vase **vases**
You put flowers
in a **vase**.

vegetable **vegetables**
A **vegetable** is a plant that you
grow for food. Potatoes, carrots, and
peas are all **vegetables**. Salad is
made with raw **vegetables**.
For dinner today we had meat with roast
potatoes and two other vegetables.

vehicle **vehicles**
Any machine that you can travel
around in or on is a **vehicle**. Cars,
buses, vans, and bicycles are all
vehicles.

verb **verbs**
A **verb** is a word that says what is
happening or being done.

The birds sang
as Patrick (walked) to school.
(verbs)

verse **verses**
A **verse** is a group of lines of a poem
or a song, like this:
Here we go round the mulberry bush,
The mulberry bush, the mulberry bush,
Here we go round the mulberry bush,
On a cold and frosty morning.

a b c d e f g h i j k l m n o p q r s t u **Vv** w x y z

a
b
c
d
e
f
g
h
i
j
k
l
m
n
o
p
q
r
s
t
u

Vv

w
x
y
z

vet **vets**

A **vet** looks after sick animals.
*When our puppy was sick, the **vet** gave her some pills to make her better.*

video **videos, videoing, videoed**

1 A **video** is a tape with TV programs or films recorded on it. You play a **video** on a **video** recorder and watch it on a television.
2 If you **video** something, you record pictures and sounds on tape.
3 A **video** camera records moving pictures and sound.

village **villages**

A **village** is a group of streets and houses. It is smaller than a town.

violin **violins**

A **violin** is a musical instrument made of wood. You play it by holding it under your chin and pulling a stick called a bow across the strings.

visible

If something is **visible**, you can see it.
*I'm just **visible** behind my mom in this photo.*

visit **visits, visiting, visited**

When you **visit** people, you go to see them at their home.

visitor **visitors**

A **visitor** is someone who comes to visit you.
*We've got **visitors** coming to stay this weekend.*

voice **voices**

Your **voice** is the sound you make when you speak.
*I caught a bad cold and lost my **voice**.*

volcano **volcanoes**

A **volcano** is a mountain that sometimes throws smoke and melted rocks into the sky.

vote **votes, voting, voted**

You **vote** for someone or something by saying which you choose.
*We **voted** to buy a hamster as a class pet.*

vowel **vowels**

The **vowels** are the letters a, e, i, o, u, and simetimes y. The other letters are consonants.

wagon wagons

A **wagon** is used to carry heavy things. It is usually pulled by horses.

waist waists

Your **waist** is the middle part of your body. (See page 174.)

wait waits, waiting, waited

If you **wait** for something, you don't do something until it happens.
I am waiting for Kyle to help me.

wake wakes, waking, woke, woken

You **wake** up when you stop being asleep.

walk walks, walking, walked

You **walk** by putting one foot in front of the other. **Walking** is slower than running.

wall walls

A **wall** of a building or room is one of its sides.
I'll hang your picture on the wall.

wand wands

Magicians or wizards use a small stick called a **wand** when they do magic tricks.

want wants, wanting, wanted

If you **want** something, you would like to have it.
Bethany wants a banana.

war wars

When countries go to **war**, their armies fight each other.

wardrobe wardrobes

1 A **wardrobe** is a large cabinet for keeping clothes in.

2 All your clothes make up your **wardrobe**.

warm warmer, warmest

Warm means quite hot but not very hot.
This bread is still warm from the oven.

warn warns, warning, warned

You **warn** someone by telling them about something bad that might happen.
The weatherman warned us of storms and rain.

warning warnings

A **warning** tells you that there is something bad or dangerous.
The notice said: "Warning: fog."

wash washes, washing, washed

You **wash** yourself with water to make your skin clean.

washing machine washing machines

A **washing machine** is a machine that washes clothes.

a b c d e f g h i j k l m n o p q r s t u v **Ww** x y z

a
b
c
d
e
f
g
h
i
j
k
l
m
n
o
p
q
r
s
t
u
v

Ww

x
y
z

wasp wasps
A **wasp** is an insect with black and yellow stripes. It stings.

waste wastes, wasting, wasted
When you **waste** something, you do not use it well.
You've wasted an hour finding your pen.
This food will be wasted if no one eats it.

watch watches, watching, watched
1 A **watch** is a small clock you wear on your wrist.
2 You **watch** someone by looking at them to see what they are doing.

water
Water falls from the sky as rain. It flows down rivers to the sea.

waterproof
If something is **waterproof**, it does not let in water.
Bring a waterproof coat in case it rains.

wave waves, waving, waved
1 You **wave** to someone by raising your arm and moving it about.
2 A **wave** is also a raised line of water that moves across the sea.
The surfer rode on a huge wave.

wax
Wax is a material. It is used to make candles and crayons. **Wax** melts when it is heated.

way ways
1 If you tell someone the **way**, you say how to get to a place.
2 The **way** to do something is how to do it.
This is the way to throw the ball.

weak weaker, weakest
Weak means not strong.
I ran up the hill till my legs felt weak.

wear wears, wearing, wore, worn
1 When you **wear** clothes, you have them on.
Ryan's wearing jeans today.
2 When something is **worn** out, it cannot be used anymore.

weather
Rain, sunshine, storms, and snow are different kinds of **weather**.
What's the weather like today?

web webs
A spider makes a **web** using threads that it makes in its body.
Spiders make webs to trap insects.

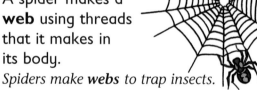

website websites
You look at a **website** on the internet to find information.

wedding weddings
When two people get married, it is their **wedding** day.

Wednesday **Wednesdays**
Wednesday is the day of the week
between Tuesday and Thursday.

weed **weeds**
A **weed** is a wild plant that people
do not want in their gardens.

week **weeks**
A **week** is made up of seven days.
There are 52 **weeks** in a year.

weekend **weekends**
Saturday and Sunday are called the
weekend.

weigh **weighs, weighing,
weighed**
Something that **weighs**
a lot is hard to
lift or carry.
*An elephant
weighs much
more than
a mouse.*

weight
The **weight** of something is how
much it weighs.

well **better, best; wells**
1 If you do something **well**, you do a
good job.
2 If you are **well**, you are healthy.
3 People get water out of a
deep hole in the ground called
a **well**.

went See **go**.

west
West is the direction you look to
see the sun set.

wet **wetter, wettest**
1 Something that is **wet** has water
or liquid on or in it.
2 If the weather is **wet**, it is raining.

whale **whales**
Whales are the largest
mammals. They live
in the sea.

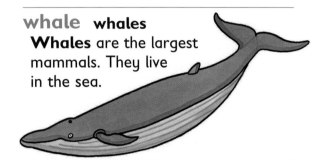

what
What is used to ask or talk about
a thing.
What is that? I can't see what it is.

wheat
Wheat is a plant grown by farmers.
Flour is made from its seeds.

wheel **wheels**
Cars, trucks, and bicycles move along
on **wheels**.

wheelchair **wheelchairs**
A **wheelchair** is a
chair with wheels.
It is used by
someone who
cannot walk.

when
When means the time at which
something happens.
When are we going to the game?

where
Where means the place at which
something is.
Where is my bag? It isn't where I left it.

a b c d e f g h i j k l m n o p q r s t u v **Ww** x y z

165

which
Which means the thing you have in mind.
Which book have you chosen? Show me which one you like best.

while
While means that two things happen at the same time.
We went skating while we were in France.

whisper whispers, whispering, whispered
If you **whisper**, you speak very quietly.

whistle whistles, whistling, whistled
1 You **whistle** by blowing air out of your mouth very loudly.
2 You can make the same noise using a metal or plastic **whistle**.

who
Who is used to ask or talk about a person.
Who put this frog on my chair?
I'm the person who telephoned you yesterday.

whole
The **whole** of something means every part of it.
Janice ate the whole cake by herself.

whose
Whose is used to ask or talk about the person something belongs to.
Whose pencils are these?
She's the girl whose mother is a singer.

why
Why is used to ask or talk about the reason for something.
Why are your shoelaces undone?
That's why you fell over!

wicked
A **wicked** person is evil. They do **wicked** things that are very unkind.

wide wider, widest
Something **wide** measures a long way from side to side.

width
When you measure how wide something is, you find its **width**.

wife wives
A **wife** is a woman that a man is married to.
My grandma is my grandpa's wife.

wild wilder, wildest
A **wild** animal or flower is one that lives without help from humans.

win wins, winning, won
The person who **wins** comes in first in a race or competition.
My team won the swimming race.

wind winds
Wind is air that moves strongly and quickly.

windmill windmills
A **windmill** is a tower with large arms that are moved around by the wind. Farmers used to use power from a **windmill** to make flour.

window windows
A **window** is a hole in the wall that lets in light. **Windows** are often filled with glass.

windshield windshields
The driver of a car looks out through the **windshield**. (See page 175.)

windy windier, windiest
It is **windy** when the wind is blowing more strongly than usual.

wing wings
A bird flaps its **wings** to help it to fly. An airplane's **wings** are fixed.

winner winners
The person who wins something is the **winner**.
*The **winner** of the first prize is Alfie.*

winter
Winter is the season between autumn and spring. It is cold and the days are short.

wipe wipes, wiping, wiped
If you **wipe** something, you clean it with paper or a cloth.
*Hayley is **wiping** the table.*

wire wires
A **wire** is a long, thin strip of metal. It bends easily and is used to fasten things. Fences and baskets can be made of **wire**.

wise wiser, wisest
A **wise** person knows a lot and is very sensible.

wish wishes, wishing, wished
1 If you **wish** for something, you want it very much.
2 When you make a **wish**, you hope to get what you want.

witch witches
A **witch** is a woman in stories who can do magic.

wives See **wife**.

wizard wizards
A **wizard** is a man in stories who can do magic.

a b c d e f g h i j k l m n o p q r s t u v **Ww** x y z

wobble

a b c d e f g h i j k l m n o p q

wobble **wobbles, wobbling, wobbled**
If something **wobbles**, it shakes from side to side.
The gelatin wobbled on the plate.

wobbly
If something is **wobbly**, it wobbles.

woke See **wake**.

woken See **wake**.

wolf **wolves**
A **wolf** is a wild animal like a large dog. **Wolves** live in groups called packs.

woman **women**
A **woman** is a grown-up female person.

won See **win**.

wonder **wonders, wondering, wondered**
When you **wonder** about something, you think about if it will happen.
I wonder if my friend will come today.

Ww

wonderful
Something **wonderful** is very good.
We've got a wonderful new TV!

x y z

won't
Won't is a short way of saying "will not."

wood **woods**
1 **Wood** is the material that comes from the trunks of trees.
2 A **wood** is a large group of trees.

wooden
Wooden means made from wood.

wool
A sheep's coat is made of **wool**. **Wool** is used to make clothes and blankets.

word **words**
You use **words** when you speak or write. A written **word** is a group of letters. It has a space at each side.

wore See **wear**.

work **works, working, worked**
1 Someone who **works** tries hard to do something.
2 When people go to **work**, they are going to do their job.

world **worlds**
The **world** is the planet that you live on and everything on it.

worm **worms**
A **worm** is a small slippery animal. It lives in the soil.

worn See **wear**.

worry **worries, worrying, worried**
If you **worry** about something, you are afraid that it might go wrong.

worse
Worse means more bad.
This film is even worse than last week's!
See **bad**.

worst
Worst means most bad.
This is the worst film I have ever watched!
See **bad**.

worth
1 Something is **worth** what you would expect to pay for it.
2 Something that is **worth** doing has a good result.

wound **wounds**
A **wound** is a cut or break in the skin.

wrap **wraps, wrapping, wrapped**
When you **wrap** something, you put something around it to cover it.

wriggle **wriggles, wriggling, wriggled**
If you **wriggle,** you move your body quickly from side to side.

wrinkle **wrinkles**
A **wrinkle** is a small fold.
Look at the wrinkles on that elephant!

wrist **wrists**
Your **wrist** is the place where your hand joins your arm. (See page 174.)

write **writes, writing, wrote, written**
You **write** when you put words on paper with a pen or pencil.

writing
When you have done some **writing**, you have written words on paper.

written See **write.**

wrong
1 Something **wrong** is not correct.
2 **Wrong** also means against the rules that people have made.
Telling lies is wrong.

wrote See **write**.

a
b
c
d
e
f
g
h
i
j
k
l
m
n
o
p
q
r
s
t
u
v

Ww

x
y
z

a
b
c
d
e
f
g
h
i
j
k
l
m
n
o
p
q
r
s
t
u
v
w

z

X ray X rays
An **X ray** is a photograph of the inside of your body. It is taken using a special kind of light.

xylophone xylophones
A **xylophone** is a musical instrument. You play it by hitting wooden bars with sticks.

yacht yachts
A **yacht** is a sailing boat. People sail **yachts** for fun.

yawn yawns, yawning, yawned
You **yawn** by opening your mouth wide and breathing out noisily. You **yawn** when you are tired.
Tom yawned and said he was going to bed.

year years
A **year** has 365 days. There are twelve months in a **year**.

yell yells, yelling, yelled
You **yell** when you shout as loudly as you can.
The children were yelling with excitement.

yes
You say **yes** to show that you agree with something or that someone is right.
"I really like ice cream!" "Yes, so do I!"
"This is your coat, isn't it?" "Yes, it is."

yesterday
Yesterday was the day that came before today.

yogurt or yoghurt yogurts or yoghurts
Yogurt is a soft, thick food made from milk. It is often mixed with sugar or fruit.

yolk yolks
The **yolk** of an egg is the yellow part in the middle.

yo-yo yo-yos
A **yo-yo** is a toy that goes up and down on a string.

young younger, youngest
A **young** person or animal has not been alive for long.

your
Your means belonging to you.
*Is this **your** coat?*

zigzag zigzags
A **zigzag** is a line that bends suddenly up and down.

zipper zippers
A **zipper** is a line of teeth that lock together to close something.

zebra zebras
A **zebra** is an animal that lives in Africa. It is like a small horse with black and white stripes.

zero zeroes
Zero is a name for the number 0.

zoo zoos
Animals are kept in a **zoo** so that people can look at them.

a
b
c
d
e
f
g
h
i
j
k
l
m
n
o
p
q
r
s
t
u
v
w
x

Yy
Zz

Dinosaurs

Tyrannosaurus rex was one of the largest meat-eaters, with very sharp teeth and claws.

Brontosaurus was a plant-eating dinosaur with a long neck and long tail.

Triceratops used its three horns to fight off other dinosaurs.

Pterodactyl lived at the same time as the dinosaurs.

Stegosaurus had bony plates on its back and a spiky tail to protect it.

Parts of the body

head

hair

ear

neck

shoulder

chest

armpit

arm

waist

elbow

wrist

nail

thigh

stomach

navel

hip

thumb

hand

palm

finger

knee

calf

leg

shin

heel

ankle

foot

toe

Parts of the face

forehead

eyelashes

eye

cheek

mouth

lip

eyebrow

nose

nostril

teeth

chin

Parts of a bicycle

saddle

handlebars

bell

light

light

brake

tire

spoke

wheel

pedal

chain

Parts of a car

roof

windshield

windshield wiper

hood

trunk

gas cap

engine

headlight

rear door

door handle

front door

tire

bumper

Clothes

bathrobe

blouse

scarf

nightgown

hat

sweater

jacket

skirt

glove

sandals

coat

jeans

tights

sneakers

swimsuit

dress

slippers

panty

leotard

pajamas

cap

jacket

collar

shirt

sleeve

boots

socks

cuff

belt

tie

swimming trunks

pants

T-shirt

underpants

shoe

shoelaces

undershirt

sweatsuit

shorts

Time

one o'clock

quarter past one

half past one

quarter to two

yesterday	second	dawn	**Days**	**Months**
today	minute	morning	Monday	January
tomorrow	hour	noon	Tuesday	February
	day	afternoon	Wednesday	March
	week	dusk	Thursday	April
	fortnight	evening	Friday	May
	month	night	Saturday	June
	year	midnight	Sunday	July
	decade			August
	century			September
	millennium			October
				November
				December

Seasons

spring

summer

autumn

winter

Words we use to ask questions

how   what   when   where   who   why   which

Pronouns

I	me	my	mine	myself
you	you	your	yours	yourself, yourselves
he, she, it	him, her, it	his, her, its	his, hers, its	himself, herself, itself
we	us	our	ours	ourselves
they	them	their	theirs	themselves

Words we use a lot

a	can't	like	should
about	come	look	so
after	could	many	some
again	did	may	than
all	do	more	that
am	don't	much	the
an	for	must	then
and	from	next	there
another	get	no	these
are	go	not	this
as	going	now	to
at	got	of	too
away	had	once	very
back	has	or	was
be	have	out	way
because	here	play	went
been	if	put	were
but	in	said	will
by	into	saw	with
came	is	see	would
can	just	seen	yes

Synonyms

Synonyms are words that have almost the same meaning.

How many synonyms can you think of?

small
tiny ...

big
large ...

tasty
delicious ...

neat
tidy ...

wet
damp ...

unhappy
sad ...

yell
shout ...

cook
bake ...

afraid
scared ...

fast
quick ...

reply
answer ...

18+7=25

Antonyms are words that mean the opposite.

sad   happy

high   low

wide   narrow

hot   cold

old   new

come   go

asleep   awake

full   empty

dark   light

inside   outside

back   front

open   closed

heavy   light

few   many

noisy   quiet

clean   dirty

soft   hard

wet   dry

fast   slow

Position words

up

down

top

first

bottom

through

above

last

below

between

off

on

beside

behind

over

far

in front

under

near

Numbers

0	zero	21	twenty-one	1st	first
1	one	30	thirty	2nd	second
2	two	31	thirty-one	3rd	third
3	three	40	forty	4th	fourth
4	four	41	forty-one	5th	fifth
5	five	50	fifty	6th	sixth
6	six	51	fifty-one	7th	seventh
7	seven	60	sixty	8th	eighth
8	eight	61	sixty-one	9th	ninth
9	nine	70	seventy	10th	tenth
10	ten	71	seventy-one	11th	eleventh
11	eleven	80	eighty	12th	twelfth
12	twelve	81	eighty-one	13th	thirteenth
13	thirteen	90	ninety	14th	fourteenth
14	fourteen	91	ninety-one	15th	fifteenth
15	fifteen	100	one hundred	16th	sixteenth
16	sixteen	200	two hundred	17th	seventeenth
17	seventeen	1000	one thousand	18th	eighteenth
18	eighteen	10 000	ten thousand	19th	nineteenth
19	nineteen	100 000	one hundred thousand	20th	twentieth
20	twenty	1 000 000	one million	21st	twenty-first

Measurement

Length
inch (in)
foot (ft)
yard (yd)
mile (mi)
millimeter (mm)
centimeter (cm)
meter (m)
kilometer (km)

Mass
ounce (oz)
pound (lb)
ton (ton)
gram (g)
half-kilogram
kilogram (kg)

Capacity
fluid ounce (fl oz)
pint (pt)
quart (qt)
gallon (gal)
milliliter (ml)
half-liter
liter (l)

Shapes and colors

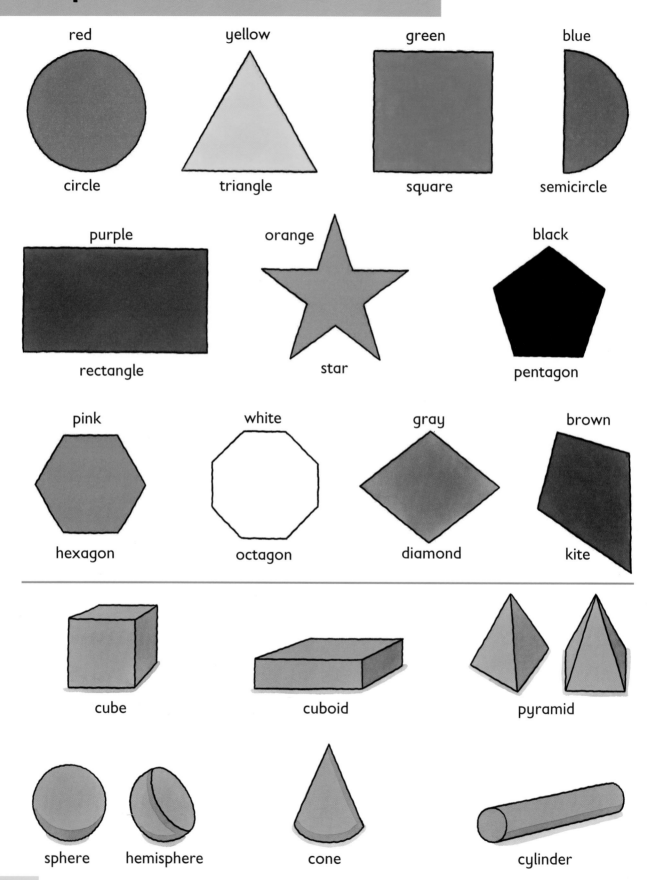

red
circle

yellow
triangle

green
square

blue
semicircle

purple
rectangle

orange
star

black
pentagon

pink
hexagon

white
octagon

gray
diamond

brown
kite

cube

cuboid

pyramid

sphere   hemisphere

cone

cylinder